The Humanists versus the Reactionary Avant Garde

The Humanists versus the Reactionary Avant Garde

Clashing Visions for Today's Architecture

by Charles Siegel

Omo Press

adolescentium alunt
senectutem oblectant

ISBN 978-1-941667-07-1

Cover photograph by Aurelien Guichard

Chapters 2 and 9 have been published, in a different form, on the web site of INTBAU, a project of Prince Charles' Foundation

Copyright © 2016 by Charles Siegel

Contents

Chapter 1: Architecture in a Technological Society 7

Chapter 2: Evolutionary Psychology and Building ... 18

Chapter 3: Beyond Modernist Urbanism 35

Chapter 4: Beyond Modernist Architecture 66

Chapter 5: The Reactionary Avant Garde 91

Chapter 6: Architecture and Culture 110

Chapter 7: A Style for our Time 123

Chapter 8: A Meaningful Skyline 140

Chapter 9: From Modernism to Humanism 148

Notes 163

Chapter 1
Architecture in a Technological Society

Architects in a technological society can support the status quo by glorifying technology, or they can challenge the status quo by humanizing technology.

Our avant-gardist architects claim they are progressive because their buildings are futuristic, but their work is really pure esthetics with no political content. They criticize the traditional architecture and neighborhood design of the New Urbanists as nostalgic and conservative, but many progressive environmentalists support New Urbanism.

The avant gardists are not really progressive politically because they do not engage a key political question of our time, how to use modern technology in more humane and sustainable ways. While the avant gardists produce flashy buildings that get all the media attention, the neotraditional designers are doing the hard work of designing buildings and neighborhoods that are good places for people—developing a humanistic architecture and urbanism.

Modernist Design

In the early to mid-twentieth century, architecture and urban design both were dominated by modernists who glorified technology, as we can see by looking at two famous designs.

Mies van der Rohe's glass and steel apartment buildings on Lake Shore Drive, Chicago (1949-1951) are typical examples of mid-century modernist architecture (Figure 1-1). This sort of boxy high-rise, with a steel skeleton and

Figure 1-1: Mies van der Rohe, apartment buildings on Lake Shore Drive, Chicago, 1949-1951. Mies' two buildings (in the foreground) looked striking when they were first built and stood in isolation, but they look oppressive now that they are surrounded by other buildings in the same style. Photo by JeremyA.

Figure 1-2: Le Corbusier, Voisin Plan for Paris, 1925. This sort of tower-in-a-park slum clearance was popular in the United States in the 1950s and 1960s, when modernism was the establishment style of urban design.

glass curtain walls, soon became the standard design for office buildings as well as for apartments. Our cities are now filled with variations on this theme.

Le Corbusier's Voisin plan (1925), is a typical example of modernist urbanism. This plan would have demolished the Marias district of Paris and replaced it with identical sixty-story towers in a park-like setting (Figure 1-2). Though the Marais district was spared, many urban neighborhoods in the United States were demolished and replaced with high-rise housing projects during the 1950s and 1960s, when this style of urban renewal was popular.

Modernist design became so popular during the mid-twentieth century because these gleaming glass, steel, and concrete buildings symbolized the technological optimism of the time. This style proclaimed that the modern era was so advanced that it could ignore models from the past and redesign society on scientific grounds. Architecture helped spread the faith that, by unleashing technology, we could heal the sick, replace the slums with hygienic housing projects, and create affluence for all.

This sort of technophilia made some sense a century ago. At the beginning of the twentieth century, the average American's income was near what we now define as the poverty level, but the economy was growing quickly. Because of rapid industrialization, per capita GNP in 1900 was almost twice what it had been in 1870.[1] It seemed that industrialization would make it possible for the masses to escape from poverty for the first time in history. New technologies and economic growth were overcoming scarcity and promising a better future.

This technophilia no longer makes sense today, because the economic changes of the last century have made it obsolete. At the beginning of the twenty-first century, average income was more than five times as much as it was in 1900 (after correcting for inflation). Because most Americans today have the basics and more, the promise that technology and economic growth would bring us the basics no longer seems as relevant as it did a century ago.

In 1900, middle-class Americans who lived in streetcar suburbs did not own vehicles; only the rich could afford to keep carriages in our cities and suburbs. Today, most American households own two or more cars, and there are more cars than there are licensed drivers.

In 1900, many of America's urban workers lived in crowded tenements, where there was only one toilet per floor, where you filled a tin tub in the kitchen to take a bath, where inner rooms had no sunlight, and where children had nowhere to play except the streets. The modernist designs for "workers housing" (and the mid-century housing projects built in their image) had windows that let natural light into every room, had a private bathroom for every apartment, and had lawns and playgrounds for the children. No one minded that these designs were standardized and impersonal; they provided the basics of a decent life, and this alone made them look good compared with the slums.

By the 1960s, economic growth had already allowed most Americans to escape from poverty. One economist became famous by writing in 1958 that America was an "affluent society."[2] Most people already had the minimum basics of a decent life, so they were less likely to be impressed by the promise that technology would bring them the basics in the future. Workers were moving to the suburbs, and they certainly did not want to live the in drab housing projects that had looked good when modernists first proposed them at the beginning of the century.

At the same time, it became obvious that technology was creating problems, such as pollution and traffic congestion. In the 1960s there were widespread criticisms of the abuses of modern technology and calls for a new focus on the quality of life, which became a major force in American politics after the first Earth Day in 1970.

Beyond Modernism

During the 1960s and 1970s, architects and urbanists were among the leaders of this new movement focusing on quality of life, and they often criticized modernism. The modernists rejected the past in favor of the newest and flashiest technology, but critics of modernism were willing to learn from the past about how to use technology for human purposes.

By the 1960s, it was clear that the modernist urbanism was making American cities less livable. Low-income housing projects, in the style of Le Corbusier's Voisin plan, had higher crime rates than the older neighborhoods surrounding them. Freeways were blighting old urban neighborhoods. Freeway-oriented suburbs were paving over the countryside, replacing it with ugly sprawl.

Urbanists led the way in criticizing the misuse of technology in mid-century America: citizen protests against urban freeways, criticisms of urban sprawl, and the obvious failures of modernist housing projects helped to burst the bubble of mid-century technophilia. For decades, this criticism of modernism was largely negative, focused on stopping freeways, sprawl, and massive urban renewal projects, but by the 1980s, it turned positive: The New Urbanism became the most important movement in city planning, and it moved beyond modernist urban design by learning from traditional models of urbanism. The New Urbanists began building old fashioned, walkable neighborhoods again, with homes facing the sidewalks and with Main Streets that have apartments above the storefronts.

Architects also began to criticize modernism in the 1960s; and by the 1970s, it seemed that modernist architecture was being replaced by a postmodern architecture that was willing to learn from traditional models. But postmodern architecture was ambivalent. It revived earlier styles in ways that were sometimes serious and sometimes ironic. Academics today focus on the ironic side of postmodernism, but this book will argue that we should be studying its serious attempts to learn from the past.

Like the New Urbanists, the serious postmodern architects were part of the larger movement to humanize technology that began in the 1960s and 1970s.

In urbanism, the movement beyond modernism has continued. New Urbanism dominates today's city planning.

In architecture, by contrast, the establishment has rejected postmodernism and has revived modernism — but in a form that no longer has its original social meaning. Mid-century modernism was idealistic and was part of a larger progressive movement for social change. Today's modernism just gets esthetic thrills from buildings that are unconventional and sometimes grotesque, and it is not connected with any larger social movement. The mid-century modernists thought they were leading us to a better society, with prosperity for all, but no one thinks that Frank Gehry and the other avant gardists are leading us to a better society.

Today, there is a split between urbanism and architecture. In the early and mid-twentieth century, architecture and urbanism fit together perfectly, as we can see in the pictures of the tower by Mies and the Voisin plan by Le Corbusier. By contrast, today's urbanists and establishment architects have very different visions, as we can see by looking at the pictures of Celebration (Figure 1-3), which looks like a neighborhood where people live, and of a Gehry museum (Figure 1-4), which looks like an avant-garde sculpture from the 1950s.

The New Urbanists are humanists who try to create good places for people, and they look down on avant gardists who are only interested in style and in flashy effects. The avant-gardist architects are esthetes, and they look down on New Urbanists who (they say) are "nostalgic" and are designing "theme parks."

Today's avant-gardist architects consider themselves progressive, but they are actually reactionary: they have forgotten the lessons of the 1960s and the 1970s and have gone back to the technophilia of mid-century modernism.

Society in general has moved beyond modernism since the 1970s, largely as a result of the environmental movement. There are only two groups in today's society that celebrate

Architecture in a Technological Society 13

Figure 1-3: Celebration, Florida, master plan by Cooper, Robertson & Partners and Robert A. M. Stern, 1996. A walkable suburb with apartments above the stores in its shopping district. The town learns from traditional models how to create a livable place. Photo by Steve Price.

Figure 1-4: Frank Gehry, Guggenheim Museum, Bilbao, Spain, 1997. The architect designs a sculpture rather than a place. This building is the icon of today's avant gardists, who specialize in icons. Photo by Ardfern.

technology uncritically. One is the "drill, baby, drill" wing of the Republican party, which knows that it is conservative to stick with the technophilia of the 1950s. The other is the architectural establishment, which has somehow convinced itself that it is progressive to revive the technophilia of the 1950s.

Today's avant-gardism is a reactionary style, a cliquish taste that ignores the lessons that society began to learn in the 1970s. It is retrograde esthetically, a revival of earlier modernist styles. It is retrograde politically, uncritically celebrating technology at a time in history when it is vital to limit destructive technologies.

Humanizing Technology

The recent history of architecture and urbanism is important because it involves a key issue of our time: How should we use technology for human purposes?

Among mid-century modernists, the design centered on the technology. The dogma was that the design must be an "honest expression" of modern materials and functions: the building expressed the technology. The modernists' designs were so striking that they helped spread technophilia through society.

Among the serious postmodernists and the New Urbanists, design centers on the human users. They are not against modern technology, but they are selective in their use of technology. They use modern technology in ways that help to create good places for people.

For example, modernists designed cities around the automobile. They had faith that this new technology would improve our lives. In any case, it would inevitably dominate our lives, because you can't stop progress. By the 1960s, it was becoming clear that the modernists' theories had created an ugly, environmentally destructive suburban landscape of freeways, shopping malls, and auto-dependent subdivisions.

The New Urbanists take a more reasonable view of this technology: they accommodate the automobile but do not let it dominate our lives. New Urbanist design centers on creating streets and public spaces that are attractive, comfortable places for people, and it accommodates the automobile in ways that further this goal. They emphasize that their traditional urbanism can work with any style of architecture, and they mention Tel Aviv and Miami's South Beach as examples of cities where good traditional urbanism is combined with modernist architecture, but their main goal is to create good places rather than to design an "expression" of modern technology.

Modernists also designed individual buildings around new technology: the buildings were "honest expressions" of glass, steel, and concrete. By the 1970s, it was becoming clear that these buildings were cold, sterile and overwhelming. Serious postmodernists tried to design buildings that were attractive, comfortable places for people to be.

Yet today's avant gardists have gone back to the sterile high-tech design of the modernists with added "artistic" pretentions. They often create very uncomfortable places for people to be.

The use of technology is a key issue of our time, because modern technology gives us more power and more freedom of choice than ever before, and we can use this power well or badly. Modern technology can be immensely beneficial; an obvious example is polio vaccination. And it can be immensely destructive; an obvious example is nuclear weapons. We need to use the beneficial technology and limit the destructive technology.

Technology also gives us immense freedom of choice, which we can use well or badly. For example, traditional agricultural societies had a limited variety of foods that grew locally, they prepared these foods in a few conventional ways, and they lived with the constant threat of hunger. Modern societies have a greater abundance and variety of foods. Everywhere in the world, people can choose to eat the corn that was domesticated in the Americas, the rice that was domesticated in Asia, the wheat and barley that were domesticated in the Middle East, the spices that were domesticated in the Indies, and a vast number of other foods that originated in every corner of the world. We can use this abundance to eat a more varied and healthier diet than any society in the past, or we can use it to eat a diet that is heavy on processed food and high-fructose corn syrup, the diet that has made today's Americans more obese than any society in the past.

It is easy to add similar examples. Modern technology lets us choose among a huge variety of drugs, which we can use to cure diseases or which we can abuse to feed addictions.

The same reasoning applies to architecture. Modern technology lets us choose among many different ways to build. Traditional societies were limited by the local materials and the relatively simple techniques available to them; their vernacular buildings were stylistically consistent because they did not have much choice about how to build. Today, we have a much greater choice of materials and of building methods. We can use this choice to design buildings and cities that are more livable than ever before, or to design buildings and cities that are more sterile and overwhelming than ever before.

The architecture establishment says we should build in styles that are "of our time" and that anyone who learns from traditional architecture is "nostalgic." They should learn from the more sensible attitude that we have toward food. The best restaurants use locally grown, fresh ingredients (as traditional societies did) because they produce healthier, tastier food, but no one says that these restaurants are "nostalgic" and that they should use mass-produced canned or frozen ingredients because industrial agriculture is "of our time."

When it comes to food, no one cares about this sort of precious esthetic criticism because we have very clear criteria for deciding whether food is good: taste and nutritional value. The best restaurants use some new technologies, such as *sous vide* cooking, but they use them because the food tastes better — not because they are "of our time."

These criteria are based on human nature. Our bodies evolved to need certain nutrients. Our tastes evolved to make us enjoy food that helped our ancestors survive during the period of evolutionary adaptation. Evolution has hard-wired these needs and preferences into human nature, and chefs work to accommodate them.

Has evolution also given us preferences about the buildings and neighborhoods that we live in? Are there aspects of human nature that architects should work to accommodate? We will look at this question in the next chapter.

Since the 1970s, the environmental movement has shown us that we must make a deliberate choice of technologies — for example, by choosing solar and wind power rather than coal to generate our electricity — but this movement focuses on limiting technologies that pose grave threats to health or to the natural environment. Architecture and urbanism could do much more. Because they design the built environment that we live in, they could help society learn how to use modern technology in ways that are in keeping with human nature.

Our reactionary avant gardists are designing the most dehumanized buildings ever built, but their approach is not inevitable. Just as mid-century-modernist architects helped spread blind faith in technology and progress, today's architects could help spread a more humanistic approach to modern technology.

Chapter 2
Evolutionary Psychology and Building

When people hear talk about a built environment "in keeping with human nature," their first reaction is often that the idea sounds very high-minded but also very vague. Yet the science of evolutionary psychology has given us many insights into evolved human nature during recent decades, and it is possible to apply some of these insights to architecture and urbanism.

Christopher Alexander, the postmodern architect and theorist, has shown that vernacular and traditional buildings all through human prehistory and history have common features that create places people are comfortable with: he calls this "the timeless way of building."[3] Modernists abandoned these timeless patterns because they were fascinated with new technology and with novelty for its own sake, so they create places where people do not feel comfortable.

Evolutionary psychology can help us understand why we like this timeless way of building and why modernist architecture and urbanism go against human nature. We must think about attitudes toward building that would have aided survival during the period of evolutionary adaptation, when our ancestors were nomadic hunters and gatherers. They built temporary structures, because they stayed in one place for only a short time, moving as their seasonal food sources changed. They built with materials found on the site, because they did not have domesticated animals to help them with hauling; when they moved, they took only the few things that they could carry by hand.

Permanent buildings developed later, beginning

about 10,000 years ago, when agriculture allowed fixed settlements. Agriculture and domestication of farm animals are relatively recent in terms of human evolutionary history. There have been some evolutionary changes since then, but these changes are not universal because they happened after people separated into different populations. For example, Europeans evolved lactose tolerance after they domesticated cows and goats, giving people who could digest milk a better chance to survive, but Chinese did not evolve lactose tolerance because they did not domesticate animals that produce milk.

To find universal principles that underlie vernacular and traditional architecture and urbanism across cultures, we have to go back beyond the invention of agriculture to Paleolithic times. Despite the immense difference between what people built then and what people built after they had permanent settlements, we can find a basis in evolutionary psychology for some key principles of today's theories of traditional architecture and urbanism.

Scale of Whole to Part

One principle of today's neo-traditional architecture is the proper scale of whole to part. Christopher Alexander and Nikos Salingaros have found that people are comfortable with buildings that have a hierarchy of scales, with a ratio of about three to one between each element and the next smaller element.[4]

For example, a large building might be broken up into two wings and a central portion, each one-third the size of the building. These three portions might each be broken up into three bays by pilasters. The bays might have windows that break them up visually into smaller areas.

Looking at traditional buildings, we can see that there is a great deal of latitude involved. The ratio can be anywhere between two and five. The submasses of the building can be unequal. Sometimes traditional buildings use more than five repeated elements, to create an effect that is imposing rather than comfortable. Nevertheless, there is a nested hierarchy of scales within the building, and for all except monumental buildings, the ratio of whole to part at each level in the hierarchy is somewhere near three-to-one.

We can speculate that we are comfortable with this sort of design, because it is based on the ratio between the structure and the entrance of temporary shelters, as we can see in the Figure 2-1.

In this nineteenth century painting of an American Indian teepee, the width of the entrance is less than one third of the width of the front of the structure. But this structure is made of hides that have been sewn together, and the needle was invented relatively late in our evolutionary history, probably about 50,000 to 60,000 years ago. During most of our evolutionary history, the structure would probably have been smaller, and the entrance would have remained about the same size, creating a ratio of about three to one.

Figure 2-1: "Crow Lodge of Twenty-five Buffalo Skins" painting by George Catlin 1832-33. The ratio of width to entrance would have been closer to three-to-one during most of evolutionary history, before our ancestors had needles to sew skins together and domesticated animals to transport such a heavy structure.

If the entrance is larger than this, the building does not offer as much protection from the weather. If the entrance is smaller than this, people are likely to knock over the structure when they are getting in and out. Our Paleolithic ancestors probably built structures that were more flimsy than the teepee in the illustration, perhaps made of branches or reeds tied together with vines that they found at each place where they stopped, creating a real danger of knocking over the structure.

Early humans and earlier hominids were more likely to survive if it felt right to them when a structure had an entrance that was about one-third of its width, so this scaling of whole to part became embedded in human psychology.

Figure 2-2 shows a very ordinary vernacular apartment building from the early twentieth century that uses a hierarchy of scales with this ratio. The building is divided into five sections. The central section is divided visually into three subsections, as are the bays. Many of the windows

Figure 2-2: Vernacular Apartment Building, c. 1920. Notice the nested hierarchy of scales, each with a ratio of whole to part that is about three-to-one.
Photo by Charles Siegel

Figure 2-3: Wheeler Hall, John Galen Howard, Berkeley, 1917. The central section is divided into seven subsections, so this building seems imposing.
Photo by Charles Siegel

within each subsection are divided into three sections. This building would seem cold and impersonal if it were just a box with plain plate-glass windows, but because it is divided and subdivided, it has a comfortable, intimate scale.

Most traditional buildings use a variety of ratios, ranging from two-to-one to five-to-one: the point is that the building is broken into sections, each section is broken into subsections, and so on until we get to the human-scale elements such as doors and windows. Yet monumental buildings often use higher ratios because they want to feel imposing rather than comfortable. In Figure 2-3, for example, the central section of the building is divided into seven subsections, and this higher ratio helps create the building's monumental effect.

Consistency with Variation

A key principle of today's New Urbanism, based on traditional urbanism, is that the urban fabric should be

Evolutionary Psychology and Building 23

made up of buildings that are generally consistent in style but are not identical. Andres Duany and many other New Urbanist planners have created urban codes and design codes that generate this sort of consistency with variation.

Why do we like consistency with variation? Early human ancestors did not live in permanent settlements. Judging from the behavior of existing hunters and gatherers, they lived in bands of about 30 to 100 people, which were like extended families, and these bands moved around in the course of the year, each going to the best locations for hunting and gathering during each season, and each keeping separate from the others so they had had large areas of land to support themselves. To avoid in-breeding and genetic disease, these bands practiced patrilocal exogamy: the men from one band took wives from other bands, who came to live with their husbands' bands. When bands came together - or perhaps when larger tribes came together for seasonal festivals, it was an excellent opportunity to meet potential mates from other bands.

The sort of temporary settlements that people built

Figure 2-4: "Comanche Village, Women Dressing Robes and Drying Meat," Painting by George Catlin 1834. There is consistency with variation because the structures were built by different individuals with the same techniques and traditions.

when bands came together must have combined individual variation with general consistency, because each family built its own shelter but all used the same materials and the same tradition of how to build. The teepee village in Figure 2-4 gives some idea of what it was like, though the structures were probably flimsier before the needle was invented.

Evolutionary psychology provides an obvious reason for why people find traditional urban fabric attractive: during the period of evolutionary adaptation, people who were attracted to these temporary settlements, with their genetic diversity, had a better chance of finding mates and producing healthy children. Thus, evolution hard-wired us genetically to like settlements that have this combination of general constancy and individual variation.

This sort of traditional fabric remained common during most of human history. From the earliest vernacular villages and cities until the beginning of the twentieth century, human settlements had fabric buildings similar in overall massing but different in detail.

This is necessarily the way that traditional vernacular settlements were built, with few available materials and a local tradition of how to build, but with small-scale construction—each family building its own house in traditional villages, or many small developers building similar buildings in nineteenth-century neighborhoods— creating variations within the generally consistent design (Figures 2-5 and 2-6).

Until the nineteenth century, most towns and cities were still built with this sort of consistency with variation, but during the twentieth century, we abandoned this timeless way of building for two reasons. First, larger scale development let us create mass-produced subdivisions with no variation at all. Second, new technologies let us create buildings that broke completely with the surrounding context, with no consistency at all.

The New Urbanists have shown that it is possible to avoid both these errors by using form-based codes, which create

Evolutionary Psychology and Building 25

Figure 2-5: The town of Sidi Bou Said, Tunisia, a traditional Mediterranean town. Consistency with variation accounts for the charm of this sort of vernacular town. Photo by Herbert Ortner.

Figure 2-6: Amsterdam row houses. The early modern economy still built towns with this sort of consistency with variation. Photo by Charles Siegel.

Figure 2-7: Seaside. Florida, Duany Plater-Zyberk planners, 1981. Form-based codes allow buildings to have the same consistency with variation that we find in traditional town design. Photo courtesy of Visit South Walton.

an urban fabric with the same combination of individuality and general consistency that we find in traditional cities and towns.

The most famous examples are walkable suburbs such as Andres Duany's Seaside (Figure 2-7). We can see from the illustration that Seaside has the same sort of variation with consistency as the vernacular Mediterranean town shown previously.

These walkable suburbs are the most common form of New Urbanist development because there have been more opportunities to develop new suburbs than to develop other types of neighborhoods, but Duany's Transect makes it clear that the same principles apply to neighborhoods at all densities, from small rural towns to dense cities.

Symmetry

A final principle of all vernacular and traditional architecture is so pervasive that it is not often mentioned: symmetry.

The evolutionary reason that we feel comfortable with symmetry should be obvious. If our paleolithic ancestors found symmetry pleasing and built themselves symmetrical temporary structures, then their structures were less likely to fall down, so they were more likely to survive.

But notice that the principle of symmetry and the principle of consistency with variation contradict each other. If there are variations within general overall consistency, then there is not perfect symmetry.

At the level of the individual building, both symmetry and consistency with variation are common. We are comfortable with symmetry, as in Figure 2-8, which shows that symmetry is used not only in monumental buildings but also in work-a-day vernacular buildings. We are also comfortable with consistency with variations, as in Figure 2-9.

Today's buildings are much larger than the temporary structures that Paleolithic hunters and gatherers built for themselves, and it seems that because of this change in scale, we can view a building either as a single structure that should be symmetrical or as a sort of village, that should have consistency with variations.

At the level of urban design, larger than the individual building, we are comfortable with consistency with variations. In some cases, traditional urbanism uses symmetry at the level of urban design to create places that are imposing and formal rather than comfortable, such as St. Peter's Square, but this is done in a relatively limited area, while the larger urban fabric is based on consistency with variation.

At the level of parts of the building, smaller than the individual building, we are comfortable with symmetry. Each submass of a traditional building is almost always symmetrical, though occasionally a large submass might be asymmetrical to give a quaint and rustic effect. Smaller elements of traditional buildings such as doors and windows are always symmetrical. These small elements are similar in size to the temporary structures

Figure 2-8: Vernacular California commercial building, c. 1890s: A symmetrical building creates a comfortable feel. Photo by Charles Siegel

Figure 2-9: Vernacular California home, c. 1890s. In an asymmetrical building, consistency with variation creates a comfortable feel. Photo by Charles Siegel

that our Paleolithic ancestors built, or even smaller, so our feeling for symmetry applies to them without reservation.

Modernism Makes People Uncomfortable

These three principles are just a first attempt to explain the "timeless way of building" using evolutionary psychology, but they do explain enough to let us see why modernism creates places that make people uncomfortable.

Most modernist architecture violates the first principle because it does not have a hierarchy of scales between the entire and elements such as windows. At worst, as in buildings by Mies van der Rohe (Figure 2-10), there are no intermediate masses between the scale of a very large building and a scale of individual elements such as windows. The architect deliberately makes the spandrels between the

Figure 2-10: Mies van der Rohe, IBM Building, Chicago, 1969-71. The building is a single mass, not broken up into smaller elements. Photo by J. Crocker.

windows as thin as possible, so the entire building seems to form a single mass.

The repetition in this modernist building goes far beyond the ratios that are sometimes used in traditional buildings to create an imposing, monumental effect. Rather than feeling monumental, the building feels sterile and inhuman.

Most modernist urbanism violates the second principle, consistency with variation on the urban scale, for one of two opposite reasons: sometimes because it has unvaried repetition, and sometimes it is completely inconsistent.

The large-scale development that became common in the twentieth century allows exact repetition of the same form over and over again. This feels oppressive in popular modernist urbanism, such as Levittown, with identical buildings that look mass-produced even if they have traditional detailing. It feels even more oppressive when the individual buildings are themselves in the modernist style, as in mid-twentieth-century urban housing projects built in the style of Le Corbusier's Voisin Plan, such as Alfred E. Smith Houses in Manhattan (Figure 2-11).

The vast variety of building technology developed in the twentieth century lets modernist urbanism violate the second principle in the opposite way, by designing buildings that are totally inconsistent with their context and inconsistent with each other. Traditional fabric buildings were consistent because there was a limited choice of materials and building technologies. But in the twentieth century, modernists did not hesitate to insert a glass-and-steel high-rise into a traditional urban fabric where it did not fit in. And when today's avant gardists build a neighborhood from scratch, they design a collection of look-at-me buildings that have nothing in common at all (Figure 2-12).

Today's avant-gardist architects violate the third principle by creating free-form buildings that lack symmetry even in their smallest elements, such as the building by Frank Gehry shown in Figure 2-13. These buildings are a rather desperate attempt to get away from the monotonous, sterile feeling of Mies van der Rohe's. Though they manage

Evolutionary Psychology and Building 31

Figure 2-11: Alfred E. Smith Houses, Manhattan, NY, completed in 1953. The same building design is repeated with no variation. Photo by Charles Siegel.

Figure 2-12: La Defense seen from Paris' Tour Saint Jacques. Our technology opens so many possibilities that starchitects can create a jumble of look-at-me buildings that are completely inconsistent with each other, quite a contrast with the traditional Paris urbanism in the foreground. Photo by Zinneke.

Figure 2-13: Frank Gehry, Walt Disney Concert Hall, Los Angeles, 2003. This sort of free-form building is less boring but more inhuman than mid-century modernism. Photo by PDphoto.org.

to be less boring than Mies' mid-century modernism, they are even more inhuman.

This sort of building, much admired and imitated by the avant gardists, ignores the first principle because it does not have a hierarchy of scales ranging from the building as a whole to human-scale elements such as windows, with the proper ratio of whole to part at each level of the hierarchy. Though it breaks up the building into random fragments, each fragment has large blank-faced areas of a single material, rather than being divided into subsections.

It ignores the second principle of consistency with variation, because it is so individualistic that there is no consistency at all between the individual building and nearby buildings.

It even ignores the third principle of symmetry. The asymmetry is so different from what people have always built that it has made Gehry into a media sensation, but as we will see, the people who use Gehry's buildings sometimes complain that the buildings are so uncomfortable that they cause vertigo.

The version of modernism practiced by starchitects like Gehry is as far as anyone has ever gotten from the long tradition of building that is in keeping with human nature, because its goal is to build sculptural icons that attract attention to themselves, rather than to build good places for people to be.

By contrast, today's neo-traditional architects and New Urbanists are reviving the timeless way of building that suits human nature. Their neighborhoods have individual variations within a generally consistent urban fabric, and their buildings have the proper scale of whole to part and (of course) have symmetrical smaller elements.

The Timeless Way of Building

This chapter is a first attempt to base architecture and urbanism on evolutionary psychology. There are obviously many principles of traditional design that it does not cover.

Some of the omitted principles can be explained easily by evolutionary psychology. For example, the Danish urbanist, Jan Gehl, has pointed out that "The most popular places to sit can be found on the edges of open spaces...," most obviously when streets or plazas have sidewalk cafes at their edges. By contrast, "Benches placed in the middle of open spaces look interesting on architectural drawings but are definitely less inviting...."[5] Why are people attracted to sit at the edges of urban spaces, next to their street walls? It is because our Paleolithic ancestors were safer from predators if they sat with their backs to a cliff or large rock, so they could see anything that was approaching them, rather than sitting in the midst of an open space where predators could attack them from any direction.

Other principles are more difficult to explain, and this book will not attempt a comprehensive theory of the evolutionary psychology of architecture and urbanism. It is just one step toward that theory.

Evolutionary psychologists generally begin by looking for human behavior that is consistent across cultures, and then they develop hypotheses that could explain this behavior as the result of human evolution.

In this chapter, we have looked at a few principles of urbanism and architecture that are consistent across cultures, and in the next two chapters, we will look at more principles of what Christopher Alexander called "the timeless way of building." New Urbanists have looked for these principles in city planning, and some postmodernists have looked for them in architecture. Identifying behavior that is consistent across cultures (as they have done) is the first step, before developing hypotheses to explain this behavior as the result of human evolution.

The next two chapters will begin by looking at how modernist urbanism and architecture ignored these timeless principles by developing designs that center on new technologies. Then they will look at how critics of modernism tried to reestablish these principles by going back to traditional models that have a long history of creating good places for people to be.

Chapter 3
Beyond Modernist Urbanism

Modernist urbanism centered on two new technologies: it designed large single-purpose land uses for modern industry and large high-speed roads for automobiles. During the early to mid-twentieth century, modernists embraced the ideal of building the city as a collection of large single-function areas, each surrounded by wide arterial streets or freeways.[6]

By the 1960s, this modernist ideal was coming true. But as freeways, housing projects, and sprawl suburbs were built in American cities, people began to realize that the dream had failed: the freeways blighted urban neighborhoods and generated more traffic, the housing projects became worse than the old slums that they replaced, the sprawl was paving over the countryside with strip malls and parking lots. In the 1960s and 1970s, there was a powerful political movement to stop freeways and slum-clearance housing projects.

By the 1980s, the movement to stop modernist urbanism turned into a movement to build traditional urbanism. The New Urbanists began building new suburbs and towns that look something like the old streetcar suburbs built before World War I. Environmentalists are attracted by the New Urbanism because it builds compact walkable neighborhoods, helping to protect open space from sprawl and to reduce emissions from automobiles. The public is attracted by the New Urbanism because it builds attractive, human-scale communities, instead of impersonal subdivisions and malls.

The New Urbanism has been successful at developing a more humanistic urbanism to replace modernist urbanism.

Cities for the Machine Age

Some of the most famous modernist architects developed striking visions of the city, which display the modernist urban ideal in pure form.

We have already looked at Le Corbusier's 1925 Voisin plan to replace a neighborhood in central Paris with towers in a park.

In 1924, Le Corbusier designed what he called the Radiant City (*Ville Radieuse* in French), a plan to build an entire city in this style (Figure 3-1), with office towers in the center surrounded by rings of housing slabs in park-like blocks. The blocks were surrounded by arterial streets, where pedestrians were relegated to overpasses so they would not interfere with traffic.

Figure 3-1: Le Corbusier's Radiant City, 1924. An early vision of the modernist city, made up of office towers and housing slabs surrounded by high-speed streets.

In the same vein, Walter Gropius and Marcel Breuer developed a plan for housing in 1924 that consisted of twelve-story slab apartment buildings that were parallel to each other and perpendicular to the road, with landscaped areas between them, a plan that was imitated by many mid-century housing projects.

Sigfried Giedion

Though he is less well known, Sigfried Giedion was instrumental in spreading these ideas in America. From its inception in 1928, Giedion was the secretary-general of the Congrès Internationale d'Architecture Modern (International Congress of Modern Architecture), the main group that popularized modern architecture and urbanism. Like Gropius and Breuer, Giedion left Germany after the Nazis came to power. He became a teacher at Harvard's graduate school of design and ultimately its chairman. His book, *Space, Time and Architecture* (1941) spread the ideals of modernist architecture and urbanism to a generation of students. Though most of his book focused on architecture, its section about city planning is the best single summary of modernist city planning.

Giedion believed that planning must be based on what he called the "great scale" of modern technology. Factories were becoming larger and were being located in large areas set aside for industry, isolated from housing and other land uses. Modernists believed that this same scale should be used for all the functions of the city.

Thus, the "superblock," much larger than a traditional urban block, would be the primary unit of modern planning. Civic centers, industrial parks, office parks, housing projects, and centers for the performing arts would all be built in their own single-function superblocks, so each could be designed as a unified whole. Automobile traffic would be rationalized on freeways and arterial streets, which would surround the city's superblocks, defining them visually and separating their functions. Streets and walkways within each superblock would be designed for local access, while the parkways and arterial streets would carry all through traffic

The theory was that separating land uses in this way would let each serve its purpose more efficiently. For example, in older cities, there was through traffic on residential and business streets: the cars made the streets less safe and less pleasant for people who lived and worked there, and the people slowed down traffic when they crossed the street or parked their cars at the curb. The city would function much more efficiently if there were separate freeways and arterial streets for through traffic, separate superblocks for housing and for business, and separate off-street parking. Then residents and workers would not be disturbed by traffic, and traffic would not be slowed down by pedestrians or by drivers parking.

Separating uses also made it possible for the superblocks and the roads to be designed by experts. Just as industrial engineers could design modern factories that were more efficient than the small workshops of the past, traffic engineers could design roads more efficiently, a new set of experts called housers could design housing more efficiently, and other experts could define other types of superblocks more efficiently than the mixed-use urban neighborhoods of the past.

According to the functionalist esthetic, the beauty of the city lay in its clear and honest expression of the technological reality of modern times. Buildings were abstract sculptures expressing their functions, which could be appreciated as esthetic objects because they stood in park-like open space. The city as a whole, with its superblocks and transportation corridors, had the clarity of a flowchart.

Parkways for cars were one of the first large-scale features of the modern city to appear, and Giedion thought that the city's other functions should be organized in superblocks on the same scale, saying that "the use of a new and larger scale in town planning which would coincide with the scale already being used in the parkway system is an imperative necessity for the salvation of the city."[7]

Practical Planning

Giedion and other advocates of the international style generally believed in high-rise cities, but at the same time another school of planners, the garden city planners, was working to develop lower density suburbs.

Though these two schools of planners often debated about density, their similarities are more striking than their differences in retrospect. The garden city planners wanted to separate land uses in single-function zones, at first to protect residences from factories, and later to protect residences from businesses and traffic. They wanted the residential zones to have twisting street or cul-de-sacs. Both schools wanted single-function zones with internal streets designed purely for local access; both wanted the through traffic to be on arterial streets and freeways that separated these single-function zones.

Practical planners tended to focus on these common features of the planned city and to ignore the debates between the international style planners and the garden city planners about density and scale.

For example, Clarence Perry, a practical houser, developed the very influential "neighborhood unit formula" (Figure 3-2) in his 1939 book, *Housing for the Machine Age*. He said that a neighborhood unit should be built as a superblock with an elementary school in the center. Its internal street system should be "designed to facilitate circulation within the unit and to discourage its use by through traffic," and "the unit should be bounded on all sides by arterial streets, sufficiently wide to facilitate its by-passing ... by through traffic."[8] These wide arterial streets would also define the neighborhood visually.[9] Within the unit, there would be housing in a park-like setting, and shopping would be restricted to the arterial streets at the edge of the superblocks.

Perry adopted the ideal of building park-like superblocks surrounded by wide arterial streets, which was common to the international style planners and the garden-city planners, and he ignored their disputes about density. He recommended a continuum of increasing densities, from

40   *Humanists versus Reactionary Avant Garde*

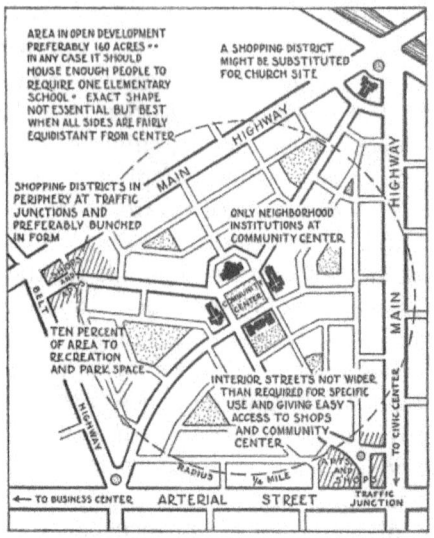

Figure 3-2: Clarence Perry's Neighborhood Unit, from the New York Regional Survey, Vol 7. 1929. The neighborhood unit contained only housing and neighborhood institutions such as churches and an elementary school. It was surrounded by highways and arterial streets, while its internal streets were designed for local access. Shopping was on the arterial streets.

suburbs to high-rises, as you moved from the outskirts to the center of the city.[10]

The Failure of Modernism

The modernist city sounded good in theory. At a time when people had great faith in technological progress, it seemed like common sense to say the city would be more efficient if it were divided into large functional areas designed by specialists with the expertise to design better transportation, better housing, and better industrial parks, centers for the arts, and the like.

Beyond Modernist Urbanism

But after World War II, when American cities were rebuilt following these theories, it became clear that they created massive problems. Perry's park-like superblocks surrounded by wide arterial streets with shopping looked good on the drawing board, but looked much less appealing when it was actually built as suburban tract housing surrounded by arterial streets connecting to malls and office parks.

Modernist urbanism was exploded by Jane Jacobs' 1961 book, *The Death and Life of Great American Cities*.[11] This is probably the most influential book ever written about city planning, because everyone was beginning to see the defects in post-war urban development, and this book was the first to describe them clearly.

Jacobs pointed out that single-function zones do not promote the street life and the network of human connections that exist in traditional mixed use neighborhoods, which have many eyes on the street to deter crime, and which have public characters such as shop owners who have a stake in promoting safety and order. This lack of community is a major reason why housing projects in the modernist style proved to have higher crime rates than older neighborhoods nearby.

Jacobs also pointed out that single-function zones surrounded by wide arterial streets make it difficult to provide adequate transportation and shopping. These single function zones are used by people who are on the same schedule, which means that they use their streets, parking lots, and nearby services at the same time. For example, at a suburban office park, the employees arrive at 9 AM, have lunch at midday, and leave at 5 PM on weekdays. Its streets are congested during these peak hours, but they are underused at other times. Its parking lots are full on weekdays, but they are empty on weekends and evenings. Nearby restaurants are overcrowded during lunch hour, but they are empty at other times. Near this office park, there might be a suburban cultural center, which draws people primarily on weekends and evenings; here the access roads and parking lots are overcrowded during events, at just the times when the office park's access roads and parking lots are empty.

Traditional cities that mix functions work much better. Mixed functions reduce peaking, so streets, parking, and nearby restaurants are used more evenly during the day and evening and during weekdays and weekends. Mixed functions give you a much greater diversity of restaurants and stores, because there are shoppers at all hours. It is very hard for a restaurant or store to be profitable based on just the lunch-time business of office workers, so areas with just offices have a few standardized restaurants and stores, which pack in as many people as possible during lunch hour to make up for the fact that they are empty the rest of the time. Mixed functions provide customers during more hours of the day and week, so they can support more diverse restaurants and stores.

The new suburbs also made it difficult for people to get anywhere by walking; they require one car for every adult and even for every teenager. Because their neighborhoods

Figure 3-3: Large blocks do not work well for pedestrians. This suburban office park has a pedestrian path winding through its two superblocks, but the city put up signs to prevent the pedestrians from crossing the arterial street. Pedestrians have to go out of their way to get to an intersection. Photo by Charles Siegel.

were made up of twisty streets or cul-de-sacs surrounded by wide arterials, the route to shopping was generally too far to walk even if you lived close to the strip mall. The strip malls themselves were ugly and dangerous places to walk, with high-speed traffic cutting across the sidewalk to reach the parking lots. The large blocks often made pedestrians go out of their way to get to intersections (Figure 3-3). Even in dense modernist developments, where it is physically possible to walk, the streetscape is so bleak that few people want to walk.

The new suburbs also paved over the open countryside. In 1958, W. H. Whyte invented the phrase "urban sprawl" and said, "huge patches of once green countryside have been turned into vast, smog-filled deserts … and each day … more countryside is being bulldozed under. You can't stop progress, they say, yet much more of this kind of progress and we shall have the paradox of prosperity lowering our real standard of living."[12] Whyte emphasized the high cost of roads and utilities and the loss of recreational land and farmland to sprawl. Today, we also can see that sprawl also contributes to global warming: it requires people to drive long distances in the course of their everyday activities, and vehicles are second only to power plants as a source of greenhouse gas emissions in the United States.

The People Against Modernism

Housing projects and urban freeways, two elements of the modernist city that were built in densely populated areas, were so obviously destructive that they inspired citizen revolts among residents who were affected.

Urban housing projects replaced functioning, mixed-use neighborhoods with sterile, single-use superblocks. Jane Jacobs pointed out that, in addition to removing large numbers of businesses, they blighted businesses on surrounding streets, because they just included housing and people no longer walked in their direction to go shopping. Because they lacked store owners and other public characters, because they lacked eyes on the street, and because they lacked public life and sense of community, they had higher crime rates than the older slum neighborhoods that they replaced.[13]

Urban freeways generally demolished large swaths of existing housing and replaced them with massive structures that made it harder for people to walk around their neighborhoods. It soon became clear that the freeways did not solve traffic problems, as promised. Freeways caused what planners call "induced demand": they encouraged more people to move out to the suburbs and to drive longer distances to shop, and so they generated new traffic that quickly filled their new capacity. One study in California, for example, found that within five years after a major freeway is built, 95% of the new capacity fills up with traffic that would not have existed if the freeway had not been built.[14]

Demolishing the Projects

The Pruitt-Igoe housing project in St. Louis (Figure 3-4) was hailed as a model of modern slum clearance when it was built in 1956. Its occupancy peaked in 1957 at 91% and then declined as residents fled from the vandalism, crime and gang violence that plagued the project. In 1968, the federal Department of Housing began to encourage the remaining residents to leave, and in 1972, HUD began demolishing the project (Figure 3-5). Ultimately, the failure of modernist housing projects became so obvious that the federal government spent $5.8 billion between 1992 and 2005 on the HOPE VI program, which demolished hundreds of modernist projects and replaced them with something more like traditional mixed-use neighborhoods, because there was no other remedy for their social failure and their high-crime rates.[15]

Stopping Freeways

The freeway revolts that spread across the nation during the 1960s and 1970s began in San Francisco. California was

Beyond Modernist Urbanism

Figure 3-4: Minoru Yamasaki, Pruitt-Igoe Housing Project, St. Louis, 1956, aerial view in 1968. Many blocks of a slum were replaced with thirty-three identical 11-story buildings in a supposedly park-like superblock. Notice how sharply the scale of the project contrasts with the the older neighborhood around it.

Figure 3-5: The famous images of Pruitt-Igoe being demolished in 1972. The critic, Charles Jencks, wrote, "Modern Architecture died in St. Louis, Missouri on July 15, 1972 … when the infamous Pruitt-Igoe scheme, or rather several of its slab blocks, were given the final *coup de grace* by dynamite."[16]

a leader of the post-war freeway binge, and the California Division of Highways and San Francisco Planning Department came up with a number of plans to crisscross San Francisco with freeways (Figure 3-6). In 1951, the city adopted what it called the Trafficways Plan and began building. Two freeways on industrial land south of Market St. were built without much controversy.

Then, in 1953, the city began building the Embarcadero freeway along a heavily used part of the city's waterfront. At this point, as freeway construction moved north of Market St. into the city's downtown and neighborhoods, opposition in the neighborhoods that were in the path of freeway construction set off the most powerful neighborhood movement that the city had ever seen. Finally, in 1959, after neighborhood groups presented them with petitions signed by 30,000 people, the Board of Supervisors voted to cancel seven of the ten planned freeways in the city, including the Embarcadero freeway—the first time in history a government body voted to stop freeways.

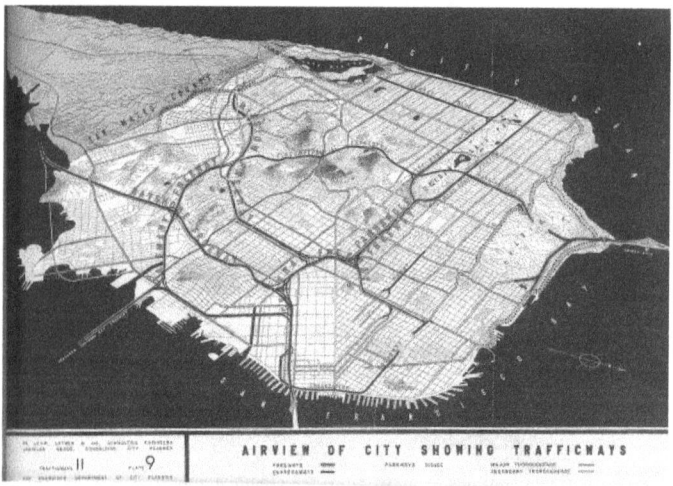

Figure 3-6: A 1948 plan to crisscross San Francisco with freeways. Most of the proposed freeways were stopped by a citizen revolt.

The city had already built small parts of the Embarcadero Freeway and the Central Freeway north of Market Street, which remained for decades, until the Embarcadero Freeway was removed in 1991, and the Central Freeway was removed in 1999. In both cases, the freeway removals caused powerful economic revivals of the surrounding neighborhoods.[17]

Fighting Robert Moses

The citizen revolts against freeways and housing projects were fiercest in New York, because there was a very visible villain to fight against: Robert Moses. By the end of World War II, Moses was the head of twelve city and state agencies, including virtually all the agencies in charge of bridges, tunnels, highways, and slum clearance.[18] He also effectively controlled the City Planning commission[19] and Housing Authority.[20]

Though he held no elective office, Moses had vast power to redesign the New York metropolitan area to suit the ideal he had learned from the modernists. He built 627 miles of super-highways in and around New York City,[21] displacing hundreds of thousands of city residents to clear the rights of way. He deliberately encouraged suburban sprawl in the outlying areas that these freeways served; for example, while he was working on the Long Island parkway system, he convinced many of the island's towns to adopt their first zoning ordinances, and he later bragged that a two-hundred-acre Long-Island farm that he had helped to develop "is now the heart of Levittown, with 80,000 residents where there were 40 or 50."[22]

Modernists admired Robert Moses. Sigfried Giedion wrote that Moses' Henry Hudson Parkway and his Long Island parkways "will constitute the forerunner of the city on a new scale."[23] The people whose homes, businesses and parks were in the way of his proposed projects felt very differently.

The first resistance was against his 1952 plan to change the road in Manhattan's Washington Square Park into an

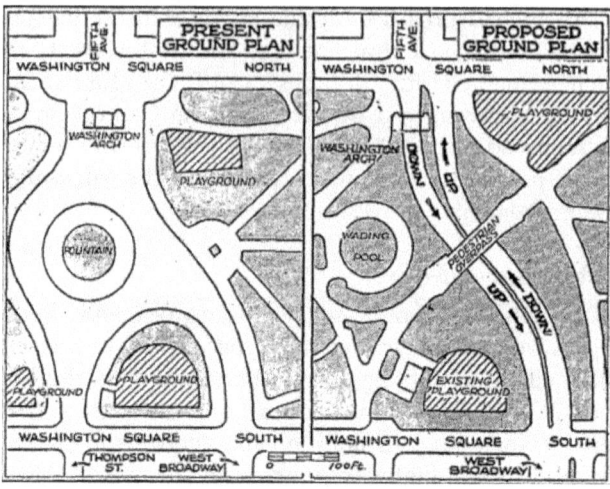

Figure 3-7: Robert Moses' plan for an expressway through Washington Square Park (right). Pedestrians would have had to use an overpass to get from one half of the park to the other.

expressway to connect Fifth Avenue (north of the park) with arterial streets that he planned as part of an urban renewal project south of the park (Figure 3-7). A local resident, Shirley Hayes, organized Save the Square to stop this plan, and advocated closing the existing streets through the park without widening the streets around it. Jane Jacobs, Eleanor Roosevelt, and many others supported Hayes' group. After massive support at a public hearing in 1958, the city closed these streets for a temporary trial. The traffic engineers had predicted unbearable congestion if the city closed these streets without widening the streets that went around the park, but in fact, there was no noticeable traffic problem. Because the trial was successful, the city closed the streets through the park permanently in 1959.

Citizen protests also stopped Moses' plans for cross-Manhattan expressways. His two freeways in Manhattan, the West Side Highway and the East River Drive, were both at the edge of the island, but these proposed cross-town expressways would have sliced through its urban fabric. By 1962, he had developed plans for a Lower Manhattan Expressway (LOMEX) that would have removed 1,972 apartments and 804 businesses to clear land for the right of way. Jane Jacobs helped to lead the fight against this project, which included rallies and demonstrations as well as massive turnouts at public hearings. After a six-hour session, city officials voted unanimously to block the project, and one assemblyman said, "I think it is time for this stubborn old man [Robert Moses] to realize that too many of his dreams turn out to be nightmares for the city."[24] The "slum" that this project would have removed has since been named SoHo, because it is south of Houston Street, its classic loft buildings have been converted into stores with housing above, and it has become one of the most popular shopping and residential districts in Manhattan (Figure 3-8).

Figure 3-8: Buildings on Broome St., on the proposed right-of-way of the Lower Manhattan Expressway. The "slum" that Robert Moses wanted to demolish has become a very successful neighborhood. Photo by Charles Siegel.

Fighting Slum Clearance

Citizen protests, led by Jacobs, also stopped the West Village Urban Renewal Plan, spearheaded by Moses' protégé James Felt, chair of the City Planning commission. This "slum clearance" project could have demolished a neighborhood of fourteen square blocks with 1,765 residents and over 80 businesses. Jacobs later recalled that she took an administrator for the Federal Housing and Home Finance Agency to see this neighborhood, and "He was floored, couldn't believe the great range of incomes. Said it was wonderful."[25] This West Village neighborhood is now considered one of the most charming parts of New York.

After defeating Moses' plan, the West Village Committee, led by Jacobs, came up with a modest plan in 1962 to build housing on some vacant lots in the area. Though Jacobs was dissatisfied with the final project, which city authorities delayed for twelve years and stripped of design amenities

Figure 3-9: West Village Houses, New York, 1962-1974. This project rejected towers in the park in favor of postmodern urbanism, oriented to the sidewalk, but the city government stripped down the architecture so it resembles modernist projects. Photo by Charles Siegel.

such as mansard roofs, these buildings are an early example of postmodern urbanism. As you can see in Figure 3-9, they fit into the street system and include a corner store. Though their architecture was reduced to modernist boxes, their urbanism moved beyond the modernist towers in a park to more traditional urban design.

Though Robert Moses was the best known villain, similar citizen battles against freeways and slum clearance were widespread during the 1960 and 1970s.

In the United States, many young planning school graduates called themselves "advocate planners" and worked with community groups to protect neighborhoods threatened by modernist projects. Paul Davidoff invented the term "advocate planner" in his 1965 essay, "Advocacy and Pluralism in Planning," where he argued that planning was political rather than value-neutral, and he called on planners to help groups that were not represented in the planning process.[26] Many professionals followed his lead: for example, in 1966, Robert Goodman, an architecture professor at MIT, began working with a group of architects and city planners to provide technical support for neighborhood groups fighting against urban renewal in Boston and against a freeway in Cambridge. They had so many requests for help from other cities that they formed a group named Urban Planning Aid and got grants to expand their work to other cities.[27]

There were similar efforts across the United States and also in Western Europe. In Brussels, Maurice Culot led a group called ARAU (Atelier de Recherche et d'Action Urbain) which fought a dozen battles to stop modernist developments by designing counter-proposals that respected their context and by organizing the affected neighborhoods to get the attention of the press. Similar protests stopped redevelopment of Covent Garden in London.[28] Redevelopment of the Nieumarkt area in Amsterdam was stopped after protests led to riots there in 1975.[29]

New Urbanism

Despite occasional projects such as West Village Houses, the movement against freeways and slum clearance during the 1960s and 1970s was primarily negative. It opposed modernist projects that threatened existing neighborhoods. It did not develop new methods of urban design to replace modernism.

In the 1980s, however, the New Urbanism became influential and began to design new neighborhoods reminiscent of the old neighborhoods that activists were trying to save. Jane Jacobs had convinced everyone that the old neighborhoods worked better than the modern projects, and decades later, the New Urbanists invented ways to build these old-fashioned neighborhoods in our time.

In 1993, the Congress for the New Urbanism was founded and increased the influence of the movement by bringing together a large number of urban designers who were working in this new idiom. The New Urbanism has been so successful that it has replaced modernism as the accepted method of urban design. Of course, there are still many locations that have modernist zoning laws and traffic engineers left over from decades ago, but the New Urbanists have won the battle over theory, and practice is gradually catching up.

Modernist urbanism was centered on new technology: cities were designed around high-speed roads for automobiles and around large-scale superblocks planned by experts. Modernists designed what Clarence Perry aptly called "housing for the machine age."

New Urbanism centers on creating good places for people. There is a dramatic shift from the modernists' technological designs to the New Urbanists' humanistic designs.

Walkable Streets

The New Urbanism rejects the modernist idea that cities should be made up of single-use superblocks with interior streets for local access and surrounding arterial streets for through traffic. Instead, it creates continuous street system with small blocks, with development oriented toward the street and sidewalk, and with a variety of different land uses within walking distance of each other. This sort of design works for both pedestrians and automobiles, while modernist design does not work for pedestrians.

To promote walking and to conserve land, New Urbanist suburbs are built at higher density than conventional suburbs—8 or 10 units per acre instead of the 4 units per acre typical of post-war suburbia, enough density to support some shopping within walking distance of most homes.

In addition, New Urbanist suburbs have narrow streets to save land and to slow traffic. Conventional suburban streets have 12 foot traffic lanes and 10 foot parking lanes. New Urbanist suburbs often have 10 foot traffic lanes and 8 foot parking lanes, which were typical during the early twentieth century, and sometimes have much narrower streets. Andres Duany has designed some streets as narrow as 19 feet wide, with two way traffic and on-street parking on one side: he calls these "yield streets," because when two cars meet that are going in opposite directions, there is not enough room for both of them, and one must yield the right of way to the other by pulling into the parking lane. Needless to say, these 19-foot-wide streets slow traffic considerably.

Conventional suburban streets also have wide turning radiuses at intersections, which allow traffic to make turns at high speeds. New Urbanist suburbs have tight turning radiuses at intersections, forcing drivers to slow down when they turn and giving pedestrians a shorter distance to cross.

New Urbanist suburbs have a variety of land uses near each other on a walkable street grid. Some streets have only housing, but there are also shopping streets within walking distance of these homes. Ideally, there should be transit stops within walking distance of homes and businesses.

In addition to using continuous street grids, higher densities, narrower streets, and mixed uses to make it

54   *Humanists versus Reactionary Avant Garde*

Figure 3-10: The Suburban Mall Is Designed for Cars. No One Would Want To Walk on this Sidewalk. Photo by Steve Price, Urban Advantage.

Figure 3-11: The New Urbanist Shopping Street Is Designed for Pedestrians and Accommodates Cars. Image by Steve Price, Urban Advantage.

possible to walk, New Urbanists orient development to the sidewalk to create neighborhoods that are pleasant places to walk.

Their shopping streets are designed like traditional Main Streets, with stores facing the sidewalk and housing or offices above (Figure 3-11). Off-street parking is behind the stores, so pedestrians walk by a continuous series of storefronts. These streets also have on-street parking, which acts as a buffer between the sidewalk and the traffic, and which slows traffic when cars stop to park. On this sort of street, the stores reinforce each other: after shopping in one store, people often walk up and down the street to look at the shop windows and at the other people. Of course, this design is just the opposite of the suburban mall (Figure 3-10), where the stores are set back from the sidewalk, parking is in front of the stores, and no on-street parking is allowed in order to speed up traffic — a layout that discourages walking.

Residential streets in New Urbanist neighborhoods are also oriented toward the sidewalk (Figure 3-13). Homes have small setbacks and front yards, and they have front doors and porches facing the sidewalk to make them more welcoming to pedestrians. Garages are usually in the back, with access through a driveway next to the house or through a rear alley. In some cases, there are second units above the garages, to increase density further and to provide a variety of different types of housing for a diverse population: the small rental units are appropriate for elderly people, for example, while the houses are appropriate for families. New Urbanists use the name "snout houses" to describe conventional suburban houses, which have huge garage doors facing the street while the door for people is inconspicuous (Figure 3-12); these houses are welcoming to cars but not to pedestrians.

Form-Based Codes

New Urbanists have developed form-based codes as an alternative to conventional zoning. Zoning laws are typically proscriptive, telling developers what they cannot

Figure 3-12: Conventional Suburban "Snout Houses" Are Welcoming to Automobiles But Not to Pedestrians. Photo by John Delano of Hammond.

Figure 3-13: New Urbanist Houses Are Welcoming to Pedestrians. Image by Steve Price, Urban Advantage.

do, while form-based codes are more prescriptive, telling developers what they should do. For example, conventional zoning ordinances have a minimum setback requirement; developers cannot build beyond the setback line but can set back buildings further than this line. By contrast, form-based codes have a build-to line; development must be built at the specified distance from the sidewalk.

Likewise, conventional zoning ordinances have a maximum height, but if the maximum height on Main Street is five stories, a developer could still build a one-story drive-in there. Form-based codes have both a maximum and a minimum height; Main Street might have a minimum height of three stories and a maximum height of five stories, so new buildings must fit in with the traditional scale of the street's architecture.

These codes have guidelines to define the building types allowed on shopping streets, streets of single-family houses, streets of row houses, and so on. In addition to these urban codes, which control the massing and location of buildings, many New Urbanist developments also have architectural codes, which specify materials that may be used, the roof overhangs that are required, and other design elements that give the entire development a consistent architectural style.[30] These architectural codes generate the consistency with variation that is typical of traditional design, as discussed in Chapter 2, but the styles can seem artificial when they are imposed from the outside in this way, different from old cities and towns that have a consistent style because they had a coherent culture.

Suburban and Urban Design

The most famous New Urbanist developments are suburbs that are designed like the American towns or suburbs of a century ago. Among the first to attract widespread attention in the 1980s were Andres Duany's Seaside (1981) and Kentlands (1988). These developments are striking illustrations of New Urbanist principles, because it is possible to build entire neighborhoods from the ground up in the suburbs.

Because these examples are so well known, there is a popular misconception that New Urbanism is just a method of designing suburbs differently. Actually, it is a traditional approach to the design of urban neighborhoods and small towns as well as suburbs.

Many urban projects have been proposed by New Urbanist designers. One of the earliest New Urbanist projects was Peter Calthorpe's proposal for development in Brooklyn in the form of a traditional neighborhood, with streets of urban row houses and higher density commercial streets, but this project was stopped by neighborhood opposition.[31] Another New Urbanist development with an urban feel is Liberty Harbor in Jersey City (Figure 3-14). The HOPE VI developments that replaced urban housing projects also were strongly influenced by New Urbanism. In fact, the Charter of the New Urbanism says as its first goal, "We stand for the restoration of existing urban centers and towns...."[32]

Figure 3-14: Liberty Harbor in Jersey City, New Jersey is an urban neighborhood with New Urbanist design. Photo by Charles Siegel.

The New Urbanists use the same principles of traditional urban design in urban neighborhoods as they use in suburbs. They reject the modernists' idea that we should build single-use superblocks surrounded by arterial streets. Instead, they build an old-fashioned continuous street grid with small blocks. They orient development to the sidewalk, to encourage people to walk among different uses. They hide parking behind buildings or they structure parking into buildings to create pedestrian-friendly façades facing the sidewalk.

Smart Growth

Criticism of suburban sprawl was a part of the broader revulsion against modernist urbanism that began in the 1950s and 1960s, but it was much harder to stop freeways and subdivisions in sparsely populated locations than it was to organize local citizens against freeways and housing projects in densely populated locations, where they were a direct threat to many people. The movement against sprawl had its first major success in Portland, Oregon, when citizens opposing a new freeway called in a New Urbanist planner to do an alternative design for the entire region, which ultimately led the region to develop a new sort of regional plan.

Battle Over the Western Bypass

In 1973, Oregon passed a law requiring all of its cities and towns to create Urban Growth Boundary (UGB) lines: cities had to project how much land would be needed for future development, draw a line that could contain all that development, and forbid new development beyond the line. In 1979, the Portland metropolitan area adopted a final UGB and also established a regional governing body named Metro.

The UGB was meant to protect open space, so the state law said nothing about how cities within the boundary should be designed. When the Oregon Department of Transportation (ODOT) proposed a freeway named the Western Bypass in the county where the region's most rapidly growing suburbs were located, Metro included the highway in its Regional Transportation Plan, though it would clearly promote more sprawl and auto-dependency.

An environmental group named 1000 Friends of Oregon opposed this freeway, and in 1988 it commissioned the New Urbanist planner, Peter Calthorpe, to develop an alternative plan, which was called "Making the Land Use, Transportation, Air Quality Connection" — or LUTRAQ for short (Figure 3-15). This plan accommodated population growth by providing new light-rail and bus service with Transit Oriented Development (TOD) clustered around the transit stations. It developed a computer model to measure how many trips TOD could shift from automobiles

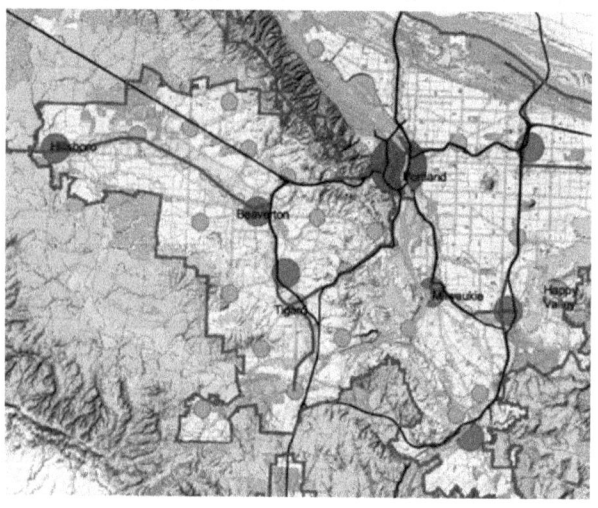

Figure 3-15: Peter Calthorpe's LUTRAC Plan, showing the urban growth boundary, transit corridors, and sites for transit-oriented development. This plan ultimately led the Portland region to adopt more environmentally sound planning practices. Image by Calthorpe Associates.

to alternative modes, which later led Metro to develop a similar model named the Urban Index.[33]

During the environmental review process, 1000 Friends got the LUTRAC plan included as one of the alternatives considered in the Environmental Impact Statement for the freeway. The EIS found that LUTRAC resulted in 18% less highway congestion and 6% to 8.7% less air pollution than the freeway. After studying the bypass and four other alternatives, the analysis found that the LUTRAC alternative was the only alternative that complied with the federal Clean Air Act. Metro killed the bypass and adopted the LUTRAC alternative in 1996.

The Region 2040 Plan

At the same time that the battle over the Western Bypass was being fought, Metro was also reviewing the UGB and developing what they called the Region 2040 Plan to accommodate projected growth during the coming decades. After extensive planning and public input, Metro ultimately adopted a plan for the entire region that was similar to LUTRAC. The 2040 Functional Plan adopted in 1996 added new light-rail, high-capacity bus lines, and feeder bus lines, and it concentrated new development around transit stops.[34] The plan also required at least eight street intersections per mile in new and redeveloping areas, requiring the small blocks that make neighborhoods walkable.

This planning made Portland a national model for smart growth. It encouraged the development of walkable suburbs, such as Orenco Station (1997), a walkable suburb built around a stop on the Westside Light Rail line at the edge of the Portland metropolitan area, with an old-fashioned Main St. for shopping, and housing within walking distance of the station and shopping. This planning also encouraged massive development of housing in the central parts of the city. For example, the Pearl District, just north of downtown, had been occupied by warehouses and rail yards, and it is now filled with new condominiums and with residential lofts in the old warehouses and is known for its art galleries and shopping.

Many other areas adopted policies to encourage smart growth. In 2008, California passed the law SB 375, requiring metropolitan regions to plan for smart growth as part of the state's effort to reduce its greenhouse gas emissions. Planning under SB 375 is still in its early stages, and there are disputes about how successful it will be; if it does succeed, then California could become known for leading the nation to build transit- and pedestrian-oriented cities in the twenty-first century, just as it led the nation in building freeway-oriented cities in the mid-twentieth century.

A New Progressivism

Modernist urbanism began as part of the progressive movement of a century ago. In the early twentieth century, when most people were near the poverty level, its faith in technology seemed justified as a way of lifting people out of poverty by promoting economic growth.

By the 1960s, most Americans no longer were near the poverty level. Rather than seeming progressive, the freeways and sprawl that modernists advocated became symbols of the failings of "the affluent society." The official goal of national economic planning was to promote rapid growth of the gross national product, but many progressives began to suspect that promoting the most rapid possible growth was not as important as promoting a higher quality of life.

The movement to preserve urban neighborhoods helped to initiate today's environmental movement. It is often said that the contemporary environmental movement began with Rachel Carson's 1962 book *Silent Spring*, which highlighted the damage that pesticides did to the natural environment, but a year earlier, Jane Jacobs' *Death and Life of Great American Cities*, was published, highlighting the damage that freeways and housing projects did to the urban environment. The environmental movement would

Beyond Modernist Urbanism

do well to recognize this part of its history. Conservatives sometimes criticize environmentalists for caring more about nature than about people, and we should remind them that the earliest environmental protests were meant to protect people living in urban neighborhoods.

The movements to protect the natural and the urban environment both resulted from a growing recognition that misuse of modern technology was lowering the quality of life. From its beginning, the contemporary environmental movement was more than just demands for technical fixes to pollution, such as lead-free gasoline and better pesticides. It posed a larger challenge to the mid-century's blind faith in technology and growth when it said that old walkable neighborhoods were more livable than the new freeway-oriented sprawl.

Protests against freeways and housing projects were among many radical political movements of the 1960s, and they used the radical tactics that were typical of the time. Jane Jacobs herself was arrested in 1967, along with Dr. Benjamin Spock, Alan Ginsberg, and about 260 others, in an anti-Vietnam-war demonstration where protestors locked arms to block the entrance to the Whitehall St. induction center.

Jacobs was also arrested in 1968 for disrupting a public hearing about Robert Moses' Lower Manhattan Expressway (LOMEX). The meeting was disrupted several times by hundreds of protesters in the audience, who shouted and stamped their feet. After about two hours, it was Jacobs' turn to speak, and she said the placement of the speaker's podium facing away from the hearing officers who would make the decision, was a sign that the officers were ignoring the public. She called on the audience to follow her as she walked up on the stage where the hearing officers were sitting. As she walked across the stage with about fifty people following her, the chairman began yelling, "Officer, arrest this woman." In the confusion, the stenographer dropped the stenotype paper she was using to record the testimony, and the audience began picking up pieces of stenotype paper, tearing them up, and throwing them into the air. Jacobs went back to the microphone and announced, "Listen to this! There is no record! There is no hearing! We are through with this phony, fink hearing."[35] Jacobs was charged with disorderly conduct and later with criminal mischief, inciting to riot, and disrupting government administration. After long delays, Jacobs pled guilty in a plea bargain, expecting to get fourteen days in jail, but instead was given a suspended sentence and ordered to pay for the damage to the stenography machine. But the disrupted meeting created such bad publicity for the project that Mayor Lindsay said in 1969 that LOMEX was "dead for all time."[36]

The New Urbanists are less rowdy, but their support of traditional urbanism over modernist urbanism is also a real challenge to our technological society. In mid-century, the freeways and sprawl suburbs were touted as examples of how economic growth would bring us a better life. The New Urbanists have shown that it is better to live in walkable neighborhoods than in these auto-dependent suburbs, implying that we should abandon our narrow focus on maximizing the rate of economic growth and instead focus on improving the quality of life.

The New Urbanists are closely connected with the environmental movement. As we have seen, when activists in Portland wanted to stop the Northwest Bypass, they went to the New Urbanist planner, Peter Calthorpe, to produce an alternative transit-and-pedestrian-oriented regional plan, and they went to New Urbanist planners to design Orenco Station and other walkable neighborhoods around the transit stations.

There has been a shift in what we mean by "progressive." In the early twentieth century, modernist architects and urbanists were part of a larger progressive political movement that believed technology and economic growth would bring a better future to the masses. Today, environmentalism is an important part of the larger progressive political movement, which believes that we should use technology selectively, controlling harmful technologies such as urban freeways, tar sands pipelines, and coal-fired power plants. The anti-freeway and anti-slum clearance movements of the 1960s and the New Urbanism that followed have been an integral part of the progressive politics of our time, and they have helped shift progressives from the technophilia of the 1950s toward the more sensible view that we should use technology for human purposes.

Chapter 4
Beyond Modernist Architecture

Like modernist urbanism, modernist architecture focused on technology. The slogan "form follows function," implied that technology should be used in a way that serves some human function, but in reality, modernists were more interested in new technology and modern art than in the human beings who used their designs.

This is very obvious if you try sitting on a few modernist chairs. Some do take good advantage of new technology; for example, there are stackable chairs that are fairly comfortable, and this use of tubular steel and molded plastic can make life more convenient. But other modernist chairs are uncomfortable to sit in because they are designed primarily as sculptural objects that show off the properties of new materials and only secondarily for their function--for people to sit on them.

Postmodernists criticized this focus on technology beginning in the 1960s and 1970s. They moved beyond modernism by making use of traditional architecture, just as urbanists of the time were moving beyond modernism by making use of traditional urban design. Yet there were two sides to postmodern architecture, as we will see: one side used tradition in a serious way, trying to learn from traditional architecture how to create good places for people to be, while the other used elements of traditional architecture in an ironic way.

The serious side of postmodern architecture designed human-scale buildings, just as New Urbanism designed human-scale neighborhoods. It was clearly an advance over modernism.

Yet beginning in the 1980s, the architectural establishment rejected this new humanism and moved back to its earlier focus on technology, bringing us the flashy avant-gardist designs that are today's elite architecture. They consider themselves progressive because they are futuristic, but the avant gardists are actually reactionaries: they ignore the lessons about the human use of technology that we have learned since the 1960s, and they regress to the focus on abstract art and on new technology for its own sake that was common in early and mid-twentieth century.

The architectural establishment ignores the serious side of postmodernism and remembers its ironic side as a historical curiosity. We will look at this establishment misreading of history in next chapter.

This chapter will look at modernist architecture and its failings. Then it will correct the establishment's view of history by showing that the serious side of postmodernism had an enduring influence, both among architects and among the public.

Form Follows Technology

Modernist architects used the slogan "Form follows function," but when we look at the earlier history of modernism and at some of the buildings that were justified using this slogan, we will see that form actually followed technology. The architects were more interested in showing off the possibilities of new technologies than they were in the human functions that their designs were supposed to serve.

Constructivism

One early school of modernist architecture was constructivism, which flourished primarily in Russia during the 1920s and early 1930s. Its stated goal was to use modernist art to serve the social goals of the revolution, but it is obvious that many constructivist architects were also

68   *Humanists versus Reactionary Avant Garde*

Figure 4-1: Konstantin Melnikov, Intourist Garage, Moscow, 1933. The building is designed as a work of abstract art. Photo by NVO.

Figure 4-2: Konstantin Melnikov, Rusakov Workers' Club, Moscow, 1927-28: The building shows off new technology that makes it possible to have large cantilevered masses, even above windows.

Beyond Modernist Architecture

celebrating modern art and modern technology for their own sake.

Some of their buildings were works of abstract art, such as Konstantin Melnikov's Intourist Garage of 1933 (Figure 4-1). Others deliberately showed off the possibilities of modern technology, such as Melnikov's Rusakov Workers' Club in Moscow (1927-28), which has large windows with solid masses protruding above them (Figure 4-2). With traditional construction methods, it would have been impossible to place such a large mass above a window with nothing directly under it to support it—much less to cantilever the mass out in this way. The building is meant to show off the capabilities of reinforced concrete.

Likewise, the Zuyev Workers' Club in Moscow, (Ilya Golosov, 1926-1928) has large masses above windows,

Figure 4-3: Ilya Golosov, Zuyev Worker's club, Moscow, 1926-1928. The architect is fascinated with new technology, and the driver passing by is in a horse-drawn wagon. Photo from the A. V. Shchusev State Research Museum of Architecture.

showing that modern materials allow designs that would never have been possible with traditional construction techniques (Figure 4-3). But notice that the picture of the Zuyev worker's club shows a horse-drawn wagon passing in front of it: at a time when people are still using this sort of crude technology, it is natural to be fascinated with the unprecedented power of new technology.

Functionalism

Constructivism fell out favor in Russia after the early 1930s, and the functionalism of the International Style became the most important school of modernist architecture. As their name implies, the functionalists claimed that their architecture was simply an expression of modern technology used to serve modern functions, so their designs were generally much more sober than the constructivists' showy use of technology.

When dogmatic modernists used the slogan "form follows function," they meant that design should depend entirely on the function and on the nature of the materials. The slogan was first popularized by the American architect, Louis Sullivan,[37] who included ornamentation in his buildings (Figures 4-4 and 4-5), but modernists interpreted it to mean that the design should be nothing more than an expression of modern materials performing a function.

They believed that adding any traditional ornamentation to this functional design was dishonest — or as they usually put it, "mendacious." They treated their esthetic principle almost as a moral principle: if you added ornamentation to the functional design, the building was completely lacking in integrity — and its architect probably was too.

The Austrian architect, Adolph Loos, put it most strongly when he said, in 1910, "Ornament is a crime." Loos compared ornamentation on buildings and on other useful objects to the tattoos of primitives, which (he claimed) show that they have not evolved to the same moral level as modern people, who would be considered degenerate if they ornamented their bodies by covering them with tattoos.[38]

Beyond Modernist Architecture 71

Figure 4-4: Louis Sullivan and Dankmar Adler, Guarantee Building, Chicago, 1894. Sullivan invented the phrase "form follows function," but this building includes applied ornamentation as well as expressing its steel skeleton. Photo by dIPENdAVE

Figure 4-5: Sullivan and Dankmar, Guarantee Building. This detail shows how elaborate the building's ornamentation is. Photo by TomFawls.

The skyscrapers designed by Ludwig Mies van der Rohe, with their steel skeletons and glass curtain walls, are considered the perfect examples of functionalism (Figure 4-6)—modern materials deployed in space to perform their function, with nothing else added. Yet postmodernists pointed out that this design is not quite as functional as it seems: it would have been more efficient to use diagonal bracing, but Mies used more expensive corner bracing in order to create a more striking image of the power of modern technology. This iconic functionalist design was not really a pure expression of the materials and function. It was a deliberate attempt to create a high-tech image.

The focus on high-tech image rather than on function is even more obvious in two steel and glass homes that are landmarks of modernist architecture, Mies' Farnsworth house (Figure 4-7) and Philip Johnson's glass house (Figure

Figure 4-6: Ludwig Mies van der Rohe and Philip Johnson, Seagram Building, New York, 1958. Mid-century modernists interpreted "form follows function" to mean that the design should be nothing but an expression of function—without added ornaments. Photo by Noroton.

Beyond Modernist Architecture

Figure 4-7: Ludwig Mies van der Rohe, Farnsworth House, Plano, Illinois, 1945-51. A steel structure painted white supports two slabs forming the floor and roof. The walls are not load-bearing and are just glass curtains. Notice the cantilevered ends of the building, showing off the capabilities of modern materials. And notice that the shades are closed most of the way to avoid letting in too much light, so the residents have no view. Photo from Historic American Building Survey, Library of Congress, Prints & Photographs Division.

4-8). High-rises with steel skeletons and glass walls are still used for office buildings, because they are more or less functional for this use: modern office buildings require large floors with open floor plans, you can span this large space with steel beams, and you can get some natural light to the entire floor with glass curtain walls. But these two famous "functionalist" homes also use glass curtain walls, though all the glass is totally dysfunctional in a home.

The functions of a house include giving residents privacy and protection from the elements and giving them access to views and fresh air. A traditional house with solid walls and windows does exactly this: the walls give you privacy and protection, while the windows let you look out and let a comfortable amount of sunlight come in. By contrast, these two glass houses give residents little privacy and expose them to uncomfortable amounts of sunlight unless they close the curtains, leaving them with no view or sunlight at all. Philip Johnson's glass house is obviously meant to create an exquisite esthetic composition, with every piece of furniture and every item on the coffee table forming an artistic whole; but unless you are obsessive, it must be very uncomfortable to live in a house where nothing can be out of place. Of course, building with a steel skeleton and glass walls is also more expensive than building an old-fashioned wood-framed house.

The designs of these houses have nothing to do with their use or with efficiency, and they have everything to do with modernists' fascination with glass and steel construction. The design centers on new technology, not on function.

This same overuse of glass became common during the 1960s in apartment buildings designed in a vernacular modernist style (Figure 4-9). The building in the illustration

Figure 4-8: Philip Johnson, Glass House, New Canaan, Connecticut, 1949. Depending on your taste, this design is either exquisitely beautiful or exquisitely boring—but it certainly is not functional. Photo by Staib.

Figure 4-9: Vernacular modernist apartment building, c. 1960. This vernacular imitation shows the failings of the famous modernist designs for housing very clearly because it lacks their slickness. Photo by Charles Siegel.

was not a luxury project, like the Farnsworth house or Johnson's glass house, so it had to be designed in a way that was actually efficient: it has a wood frame and stucco siding rather than the more expensive steel skeleton and glass curtain walls. But it does its best to have the same boxy look as the Farnsworth House and to imitate its glass walls with glass patio doors that cover the entire front of each apartment. All this glass is supposed to provide light and views, but as we can see in the illustration, the glass area is so large that most residents keep their shades closed to avoid living in a fishbowl, leaving them with no light or view at all. Some residents keep the shades open, and they have more light than they need but no privacy. Rather than arranging their possessions as artistically as Philip Johnson did, the residents ignore the fact that the building is a work of abstract art and put their possessions in places that are convenient and that make the building look cluttered.

From constructivism to the Farnsworth House to the vernacular apartment building of 1960, modernist architecture focused on new technology and abstract art, rather than on function.

In projects that had the budget, one key rule was to use modern materials, such as glass, steel, and concrete, even when wood framing was more efficient. Another key rule was to avoid ornamentation. A third key rule was to use stark, sculptural geometrical forms to emphasize the departure from tradition, rather than using traditional elements such as pitched roofs.

These rules were followed whether or not they were appropriate to the function of the building. The slogan should have been "Form follows technology" rather than "Form follows function."

The Failure of Modernism

During the 1970s, it became clear that modernism was exhausted in architecture, as it was across our culture. Critics called the period "postmodern."

In philosophy and literary criticism, postmodernism involved a rejection of "grand narratives" that gave meaning to history. Modernists had read human history as the story of progress: increased control over nature, increased economic prosperity, increased scientific knowledge, increased human freedom. Postmodernists rejected this view of history as progress, but they refused to develop another "grand narrative" to replace it. Instead, they claimed (following Derrida's deconstructionism) that texts do not have a single meaning and that many perspectives are equally valid. This combination was so popular in the universities during the 1970s and 1980s that it was nicknamed "Decon-Pomo."

In architectural theory, postmodernism had a different meaning. During the 1970s, it was used to describe designs that rejected modernism and that were willing to make some use of traditional architectural styles.

Two Sides of Postmodern Architecture

At that time, the revival of traditional styles seemed like a single movement, but in retrospect, we can see that postmodern architects actually fell into two different camps, based on two different critiques of modernism

Criticisms that modernism was cold, sterile, and dehumanized were common not only among architects but also among the public generally: for example, a famous cartoon by Saul Steinberg showed a modern office building as a piece of graph paper, showing that the impersonal architecture reflects the impersonal corporate economy. This criticism was behind the serious side of postmodernism, which tried to learn from traditional architecture how to create a new humanistic architecture.

Criticisms that modernism was boring were also common. Mies van der Rohe invented the slogan "Less is more," meaning that he created very powerful designs by eliminating all superfluous elements. These designs were striking at first, but by the 1970s, everyone was getting very tired of the steel-skeleton-glass-wall buildings that were filling all our cities, and the postmodern architect Robert Venturi played on Mies' slogan by saying "Less is a bore."[39] This criticism was behind the side of postmodernism that used traditional and popular styles grotesquely and ironically, making fun of the modernists' artistic seriousness but also making fun of any serious attempt to learn from traditional styles. This side of postmodernists seemed willing to do anything to escape from boredom, and it ultimately led to today's avant-gardism, which goes to bizarre extremes to avoid boredom.

Some of the most famous postmodern buildings mixed these two sides of the movement. For example, Philip Johnson's AT&T building in New York (completed 1984) was famous for having a pediment that looks like the top of an eighteenth-century breakfront cabinet (Figure 4-10), and it is sometimes called the Chippendale Building after the furniture designer. This pediment is ironic, and it was considered so outrageous that it drew all the public attention

78 *Humanists versus Reactionary Avant Garde*

Figure 4-10: Philip Johnson, AT&T building, New York, completed 1984, now the Sony Building. Viewed as part of the skyline, the cornice makes the ironic statement that all ornamentation is arbitrary. You can take the breakfront ornamentation used on furniture and put it on a high-rise building. Photo by David Shankbone.

Figure 4-11: Philip Johnson, AT&T building, completed 1984. Viewed from ground level, the building is a serious attempt to humanize the cityscape, a relief from the sterile glass high-rises that were standard at the time. Photo by Charles Siegel.

at the time: it implies that any historical ornamentation is arbitrary, so you might as well take ornamentation from furniture and tack it onto your skyscraper. But at the ground level, the building is a serious attempt to humanize the cityscape by providing the sort of interesting textures that were common in traditional office buildings (Figure 4-11); when you stand on the sidewalk next to it, rather than seeming ironic, it seems like a serious improvement on the sterile glass facades that were standard at the time.

The Rejection of Modernism

By the 1970s or 1980s, many architects believed that modernism was a style whose time had passed, in architecture as well as in urbanism. It seemed that modernism was a fad that had been popular for a few decades but was disappearing.

Philip Johnson himself is the best example of the change. He was famous as co-author of *The International Style*, a book based on a 1932 exhibit at New York's Museum of Modern Art, which popularized modernist architecture in America. He was famous for his glass house of 1949, which was a modernist landmark. He was famous for collaborating with Mies van der Rohe on the Seagram Building of 1958, another modernist landmark. But in the 1960s, he renounced modernism, writing in 1968, "Modern Architecture is a flop ... there is no question that our cities are uglier today than they were fifty years ago."[40]

He was a bit ahead of the curve, but by the 1970s or 1980s, most people agreed. At this time, there seemed to be a single postmodern style, but the two sides of postmodernist architecture seem distinct in hindsight, because they have led to the two very different architectural styles that are most common in our time, neo-traditionalism and avant-gardism.

The humanistic side of postmodernism led to the serious neo-traditionalism of our time, which tries to create a more human-scale architecture. This serious side of postmodernism has been forgotten almost entirely by the architectural establishment, and we will look at some of its forgotten history in this chapter.

The ironic, grotesque side of postmodernism led to the establishment avant-gardist style of our time, which tries to undermine accepted ideas of what a building should be. We will look this side of postmodernism in the next chapter.

Form Follows Human Nature

Christopher Alexander is the most important theorist of humanistic postmodernism. He wrote several very influential books beginning in the 1970s and 1980s, when he was a professor at the University of California, Berkeley, and he continues to write now, working with Prince Charles' foundation in London.

In his 1979 book, *The Timeless Way of Building*, Alexander called for a new architecture based on the common elements that are found in all vernacular and traditional architectural styles worldwide, a way of building that people are comfortable with because it fits human nature.

Alexander said that all traditional buildings were based on patterns (which Alexander uses to mean groups of rules) that gave them the quality of being alive. These patterns do not dictate all the details of a design; they generate designs that are consistent but they also allow room for variation.

For example, peasants terracing hillsides for planting follow a few simple rules, such as building the terraces along the contours of the land and spacing the terraces at certain distances from each other. As a result, the terraces are not identical but have a general resemblance. Because they all follow these simple rules, many different peasants can terrace a hillside and produce results that are consistent but varied rather than repetitive.

The same is true of the buildings of traditional villages, towns, and cities. Builders follow simple general rules for each building type, which depend on the building's function and on the materials and building techniques that are available to them. Because they follow these rules, buildings of the same type (such as houses) are not identical but do have a general family resemblance, so the entire settlement has esthetic wholeness without uniformity and monotony. Rather than being centrally planned, it unfolds organically, as new buildings are added in a piecemeal way.

Traditional patterns that produced buildings with what Alexander calls "life" — which we can call "human scale" — developed gradually on the basis of people's experience. These sorts of patterns had been the basis of most building for many millennia, but they have broken down recently, Alexander says, because they have been replaced by patterns based on the products of modern industry, such as large sheets of plate glass. We react to this loss of organic order by trying to create artificial order through centralized urban planning, mass production, and conventional zoning laws — but this does not produce the combination of consistency and variety that we find in traditional building.

Instead, Alexander says, we should consciously create patterns similar to the patterns used in traditional building, and we should test them in practice by seeing how the buildings they generate make us feel. Eventually, these patterns will become as natural to us as they were to traditional builders.

Alexander's book *A Pattern Language* (1977) codifies a large number of patterns that apply on a variety of different scales — from the design of a city, to the design of a building, to the design of an entranceway or window.

Alexander himself designs buildings in an ahistorical style that is based on these patterns but that avoids any specific traditional style. For example, Alexander's Upham House (Figure 4-12) is a very appealing building because its massing and detailing give it the same human-scale as traditional buildings, but the decorative detailing is not in classical style or Tudor style, or any other historic style. It almost looks as if he wanted to build a classical balustrade and cornice, but forced himself not to use the classical style.

Figure 4-12: Christopher Alexander, Upham House, Berkeley, 1992. The building has decorative detailing, but it avoids historical styles. Photo by Charles Siegel.

Alexander cares less about architectural style than he cares about the human-scale massing that his patterns generate. He has made an invaluable contribution by describing the sorts of forms that are needed for a humanistic architecture, but his stylistic details lack the meaning that comes from long usage and historical associations. Of course, his theory does not necessarily imply that we should build in this ahistorical style, since the traditional buildings created before the patterns deteriorated were built in the particular styles of their time.

Alexander's theory is similar to the New Urbanists' practice. New Urbanist codes are like Alexander's patterns, sets of rules that generate building designs that are varied but generally consistent. The New Urbanists, like Alexander, care less about architectural style than about the human-scale buildings and neighborhoods that their codes generate.

Humanistic Postmodernism

The widespread rejection of modernism during the 1970s led some architects to begin designing in serious revival styles, such as Alan Greenberg in the United States and Quinlan Terry in England. But the modernist sentiment that "ornament is a crime" was still strong enough that far more architects worked in a style that did not actually use traditional styles but tried (like Alexander) to learn from traditional architecture how to design buildings that were good places for people to be, with a comfortable human scale and with rich textures rather than slick glass or brutal concrete.

Because it is often ignored, we will look at a number of examples of this serious postmodern style, chosen more-or-less at random.

We can see how quickly style changed by comparing Darbourne & Darke's designs for public housing in the 1960s and the 1970s. This firm Darke became famous for designing Lillington Gardens (1961—70) in the Pimlico area of Westminster, London (Figure 4-13), a public housing project that broke up the massive, impersonal forms of typical housing projects; but this 1960s design broke up the box into blocky modernist forms, which look brutal despite their brick facades. The next decade, the same architects designed Pershore Housing (1976—77), and in this 1970s design, their rejection of modernism went further: they were willing to use traditional forms such as pitched roofs, giving the project some of the appeal of the traditional vernacular architecture of English villages (Figure 4-14). Interestingly, this project was still built on a large tract of land without a street grid, like a typical 1950s housing project (or "housing estate," as they are called in England); it had postmodern architecture but still had modernist urbanism.

A similar example of residential design, but better integrated with the street grid, is Friar's Quay (1972-5) by Fielden and Mawson (Figure 4-15). The Norwich City Council partnered with a local developer to build this

Figure 4-13: Darbourne & Darke, Lillington Gardens, London, 1961-70: This 1960s project tries to humanize public housing by breaking up the box into smaller elements and using richly textured materials, but its blocky forms still look brutal. Photo by Ewan Munro.

Figure 4-14: Darbourne & Darke, Pershore Housing, Pershore, Worcestershire, 1976-77: By the 1970s, the same architects were willing to use more traditional forms, including pitched roofs, and they actually succeeded in humanizing the architecture of public housing.

Figure 4-15: David Luckhurst of Fielden and Mawson, Friars Quay, Norwich, Norfolk, 1972-5. This project is designed in a vernacular style that harmonizes with its context, the historic center of an English town.

project on the site of a lumber yard near the historic center of their town, and it was designed in a vernacular style that fit into that context perfectly but that is distinctive because of its steeply pitched roofs.[41]

An example of office building design in this style is the Ted Weiss Federal Building (1991-94) designed by HOK, formerly Hellmuth, Obata and Kassabaum (Figures 4-16 and 4-17). This building is on Foley Square in downtown Manhattan, near New York City's most prominent courthouses, which are in neo-classical style. Though it is 32 stories high, it fits into its context by using compatible materials, by breaking up its massing as the early skyscrapers did, and by including ornamentation, though neither the building nor the ornamentation is in any specific traditional style.

This building shows how popular this sort of serious postmodernism still was in the 1990s. HOK is the largest architecture-engineering firm in the United States. It began by doing modernist designs in the orthodox style of the

86 *Humanists versus Reactionary Avant Garde*

Figure 4-16: HOK, Ted Weiss Federal Building, New York, 1994. From the distance, you can see that the building has massing reminiscent of an office building of the early twentieth century. Notice that the massing is divided into three main vertical areas, and the central area is subdivided into three areas. Photo by Charles Siegel.

Figure 4-17: HOK, Ted Weiss Federal Building, Detail. Likewise, the detailing is not in a revival style, but it does have the rich texture and human scale of traditional architecture. Photo by Charles Siegel.

1950s and 1960s. It also does buildings in the grotesque avant-gardist style that is today's orthodoxy, such as Tokyo Telecom Center (1995). During the 1990s, it was also working in the serious postmodern style.

Another typical example of this serious side of postmodern architecture is Koshland Hall on the campus of the University of California in Berkeley (Figures 4-18 and 4-19), designed by Vernon de Mars and completed in 1990. This building respects the early classical style of this campus: its early beaux-arts buildings by John Galen Howard are white granite with red tile roofs, and Koshland Hall is a white concrete with a red tile roof. It is not in a traditional style, and it has bare concrete pillars instead of classical columns with base and capital. Yet its scale and the texture of its facade show that it has learned from traditional architecture how to create the sort of place where people feel comfortable. It emphatically rejects the modernist buildings on campus, which ignore their historical context and are either slick or brutal.

This sort of design was common on many college campuses from the 1970s through the 1990s: new buildings respected their context and imitated the human scale and richness of traditional architecture without actually being in a historical style.

Neotraditionalism Today

Though this serious side of postmodernism is ignored by the architectural establishment, it has led to the two forms of neo-traditional architecture that are common today.

The first neo-traditional style of our time is what we can call eclectic traditionalism, using historic revival styles. Straight revival styles have become more common today than they were in the 1970s, largely because of the success of the New Urbanists. Many New Urbanist developments use architectural codes that require traditional styles, because this is what the market wants. This is the architecture

Figure 4-18: Vernon de Mars, Koshland Hall, UC Berkeley, 1990: The building is not in a traditional style, but it does have the human scale of traditional architecture and it respects its context. Photo by Charles Siegel.

Figure 4-19: Koshland Hall, Detail. The detailing attempts to create the rich texture of traditional architecture without using traditional ornamentation. Photo by Charles Siegel.

that the avant gardists are thinking of when they look down on the New Urbanists because their architecture is a "pastiche"—and they have a point. The New Urbanists care about good urban design, but many do not care about architectural style. Because they are using traditional styles as ornament and do not take those styles seriously, the architecture sometimes does look inauthentic.

The second neo-traditional style of our time is what we can call "the break-up-the-box style," which is probably the most common style of new residential buildings today (Figure 4-20). Like many postmodern buildings we have looked at, this style tries to imitate the massing and the human scale of traditional architecture, but it avoids any traditional ornamentation. It is very common in suburban apartment complexes and urban housing developments that are designed to have the scale and some of the feel of old-fashioned urban row houses or apartment buildings.

Figure 4-20: The break-up-the-box style is common in recent housing developments. This style is heir to the serious side of postmodernism, imitating the massing of traditional row houses to humanize the design of a large project. Fifty years ago, this sort of project would have been designed as towers-in-the-park.
Photo by Charles Siegel.

Figure 4-21: HDO Architects, Delaware Court, Berkeley, 2011. Someone is trying too hard to break up the modernist box. Photo by Charles Siegel.

Unfortunately, almost all contemporary architecture schools ignore traditional design, so architects who try to imitate the human scale of traditional architecture sometimes do not know its basic principles and come up with very strange designs. Their most common error is trying too hard to break up the box (Figure 4-21): they overdo it and produce cluttered designs, because they do not know that traditional architecture uses a nested hierarchy of scales, with a ratio of about three-to-one between each element and its sub-elements.

Chapter 5
The Reactionary Avant Garde

The histories of urbanism and architecture in the last two chapters sound very similar. In both cases, modernists reject the past and create designs based on new technology, and then people react to the modernists' inhuman designs by taking a postmodern approach that is willing to learn from the past.

The serious side of postmodern architecture was part of the larger criticism of modernism that occurred across our culture beginning in the 1960s and 1970s. Jane Jacobs' criticisms of urban freeways and slum clearance, Rachel Carson's criticisms of pesticides, the shift in public taste from processed industrial food to locally grown, natural food, and many aspects of environmentalism were all part of a widespread movement to reject the modernist obsession with new technology and instead to focus on quality of life.

The serious side of postmodern architecture, tried to learn from traditional styles how to design buildings that are good places for people. But there was another side of postmodern architecture, as we will see in this chapter, which used traditional styles in an ironic, mocking way and led to today's avant gardism.

The avant gardists have moved back to modernism — to constructivism rather than to functionalism. They are more interested in showing off what can be done with new technology than they are in creating good places for the people who use the buildings.

The avant gardists consider themselves advanced and progressive because they use the latest technology — which, in our day and age, is a bit like claiming that you are progressive because you support chemical farming rather than organic farming and freeways rather than in walkable neighborhoods.

The avant-gardist movement emerged during the 1980s, at the same time that the Reagan administration was shifting the nation to the right. Like the Reagan Republicans, the avant gardists of the 1980s were retreating from the social concerns of the 1960s and 1970s and trying to revive the spirit of the early and mid-twentieth century. Unlike the Reagan Republicans, they believed they were progressive and did not realize that they were retrograde.

They are something new in the history of art: a reactionary avant garde.

Ironic Postmodernism

The establishment's history of architecture overlooks the serious side of postmodernism, which was an attempt to reform technological society, and focuses solely on the ironic side of postmodernism.

For example, the Victoria and Albert Museum in London had an exhibit in 2011 titled "Postmodernism: Style and Subversion 1970–1990," the first major museum retrospective of postmodernism, and it included only the ironic, deliberately kitschy, postmodern architecture. This exhibit included a model of Philip Johnson's AT&T building, which showed how silly its breakfront cornice looks on the skyline but which did not give you any sense of how comfortably traditional it feels when you stand next to it on the sidewalk.

This exhibit also included the most extreme example of the ironic side of postmodernism, Charles Moore's Piazza d'Italia (Figure 5-1), a garishly colored replica of an Italian piazza that uses the five orders of classical architecture plus a sixth order with neon lights in its capitals, which Moore invented and named the "Deli Order." The columns are distorted by having capitals made of stainless steel, and having bases with their fronts cut off and replaced by flat pieces of marble. Rather than learning from traditional design how to create a coherent place, the project is made up of fragments of traditional design and is deliberately chaotic. This project ridicules the possibility of traditional architecture in modern times: traditional architecture today inevitably becomes a kitschy parody of itself.

Most of Moore's buildings are more gently ironic than Piazza d'Italia. For example, Kresge College (1972-74) at UC Santa Cruz has scale and massing that is reminiscent of a Mediterranean village, though it has flat modern forms. At first glance, it looks like the serious side of postmodernism, learning from traditional architecture how to create a good place, but it is also filled with subtle ironies. As Moore said, "it seemed important to us to establish not a set of institutional monuments to help give a sense of place to the whole ... but rather to make a set of trivial monuments, of things like drainage ditches made into fountains, or the laundromat facade a speaker's rostrum with garbage collection under..."[42]

Figure 5-1: Charles Moore with Perez Architects, Piazza d'Italia, New Orleans, 1978. The project is made up of jumbled fragments of classical architecture, plus incongruous materials, such as stainless steel and neon. Photo by Colros.

94 Humanists versus Reactionary Avant Garde

Kresge College and most of Moore's buildings, combine the serious and the ironic side of postmodernism, like Philip Johnson's Chippendale building. The difference is that everyone can see that Johnson's breakfront cornice is ironic, but Moore's ironies are often so subtle that the users of the buildings do not even notice them. They are in-jokes that let the architectural cognoscenti laugh at users who are naïve enough to take the traditional design seriously.

Michael Graves became a famous postmodern architect by designing buildings that are grotesquely ironic. His best-known work is the Portland Building (Figure 5-2). This building has parodies of columns with strange decorations where their capitals should be. It has a huge area colored to make it look like a keystone above two elements that look something like columns, which is not where a keystone

Figure 5-2: Michael Graves, Portland Building, Portland, Oregon, 1982. The main massing of the building is a big modernist box with undersized windows that make it look even more chilling. Odd parodies of traditional detailing are pasted onto the box. Photo by Steve Morgan.

Figure 5-3: Robert Venturi, Guild House, Philadelphia, 1964. One of the earliest works of postmodern architecture, this building deliberately imitates what Venturi called the "ugly and ordinary" buildings of the early twentieth century. It initially had an oversized television antenna prominently featured above the entrance, which has been removed. Photo by Smallbones.

belongs. Unlike serious postmodernism, it does not try to design a building that is a comfortable place for people: the main massing of the building is a box with small windows, which looks something like a prison, as inhuman as the most sterile modernist architecture. But incongruous traditional elements are pasted on to this box to make it less boring. In 1983, this building won the American Institute of Architects honor award,[43] a sign of how influential postmodernism was at the time. More recently, *Travel and Leisure* magazine included this building in its list of the world's fifteen ugliest buildings.[44]

Robert Venturi became a famous architectural theorist during the 1970s by saying that he liked "ugly and ordinary"[45] architecture, and he tended to imitate pop styles rather than traditional styles. His best-known project was Guild House (Figure 5-3), a very ordinary looking home for the elderly topped by an oversized television antenna;

this building mocked the artistic seriousness of modernism, not only because it is ugly and ordinary but also because the very visible antenna underlined the fact that the elderly people who live there spend most of their time watching television. Venturi also said that we should learn from the kitsch architecture of Las Vegas — and the main thing we should learn is to ignore the seriousness of modernism in favor of playfulness and parody.

This ironic and grotesque side of postmodernism led to today's avant gardist architecture, whose main goal is to subvert conventional ideas about building. By choosing to name their exhibit "Postmodernism: Style and Subversion," the curators at the Victoria and Albert museum showed that they were interpreting postmodernism as a predecessor of today's avant gardists, who love the thrill they get from playing at being subversive.

Avant-Gardist Architecture

The avant gardists' theoretical goal is to subvert conventional ideas about building. Their practical goal is to attract attention to themselves with buildings that are shockingly new and different. Both goals make them design buildings that are disorienting and uncomfortable places to be.

The members of this school are the best known architects of our time, called "starchitects" because their sensationalistic designs attract so much attention from the mass media. Their fame shows that the media is attracted to flashy novelties and cares very little about substance.

Peter Eisenman

A leading theorist of this school is Peter Eisenman. His Wexner Center (Figure 5-4), an art center at Ohio State University, is based on shifted grids that collide with each other, like many of Eisenman's buildings. Traditional buildings are based on a single grid, which means that all the walls are parallel and perpendicular to each other. By basing the walls of rooms on grids that are not parallel to each other, Eisenman creates an artsy cubist composition at the expense of disorienting the people using the building, who expect a traditional layout.

Wexner Center has some forms that recall the old armory that was once on the site, but these traditional forms are broken up so you only see fragments of them, mocking the solid feel of the old masonry building. And Wexner Center has a famous column that hangs from the ceiling but does not reach the floor, mocking the traditional notion of what a column is.

This building is on the borderline between postmodernism and today's avant gardism. Like ironic postmodernists, it uses fragments of traditional forms, and like the avant gardists, it uses a distorted version of the traditional building envelope.

Eisenman first became famous for writing obscure theoretical articles about what he called "deconstructivism."

Figure 5-4: Peter Eisenman, Wexner Center, Columbus, Ohio, 1983-1989. The broken fragments of traditional masonry forms clash with the modernist elements of the design. Inside, a column hangs from the ceiling and does not reach the floor. This sort of trick passes as profound and "subversive" in today's intellectual climate. Photo by Mike Evteev.

Just as the then-fashionable critical theory of deconstructionism tried to undermine the meanings of literary texts, architectural deconstructivism tried to undermine the meanings of architectural forms, such as columns. Deconstructivism became influential after New York's Museum of Modern Art had a 1988 exhibit entitled Deconstructivist Architecture.

The Wexner Center opened in 1989, soon after this exhibit, and the *New York Times* architecture critic praised the building, calling it "one of the most eagerly awaited architectural events of the last decade." But a *New York Times* art critic felt very differently when he reviewed the first exhibit shown there; he called the building "a spectacular failure as a place to see paintings and sculptures" because "A visitor must constantly decide where displays begin and end, what is the preferred route from one section of the exhibition to another, and where to stand for a decent look at a given work." As usual, the architecture critics love the disorienting avant-gardist design, but the people who actually want to use the building hate it.[46]

Apart from the deliberate attempt to disorient users, there were a couple of other flaws in the Wexner Center's design: the skylight leaked, and the glass walls let in enough light to damage the art works. At first, the museum tried makeshift solutions to these problems, covering the skylight with a membrane and the glass walls with curtains, but then they decided that the building needed a complete overhaul. Just a decade after it was completed, they closed this avant-gardist icon for three years to do a $15.8 million renovation.

Frank Gehry

The best known architect in the avant-gardist school is Frank Gehry, who has become such a celebrity that he was featured on "The Simpsons" television show.

Gehry became famous for designing the Guggenheim Museum in Bilbao (1997), which looks like an abstract sculpture in the avant garde style of the 1920s or 1950s (see Figure 1-4). This building was obviously influenced by deconstructivism: it distorts the building envelop by using non-rectangular shapes, and it disorients its users because its exterior is not made up of horizontal or vertical surfaces like traditional buildings. It is clad in titanium—a material that is not very practical because of its cost but that is definitely very new, very different, and very shiny.

After Gehry did a few buildings in this style, they no longer seemed quite as new and different as they used to, and Gehry branched out by designing the Stata Center at MIT (Figure 5-5), with walls that look like they are collapsing.

Because the leaning walls meet the roof at odd angles, the Stata Center had so many leaks and other structural problems that that a *Boston Globe* columnist called it a "$300 million fixer-upper." The leaning walls disorient users by making it seem like the floors and ceilings slope, though they actually do not. MIT professor Noam Chomsky said that, when he moved into his office in this building, he got

Figure 5-5: Frank Gehry, Stata Center, Cambridge, Massachusetts, 2004. Even more than in Gehry's earlier buildings, the desire to be new and different inconveniences and disorients the building's users. Photo by Tjeerd Wiersma.

100   *Humanists versus Reactionary Avant Garde*

vertigo whenever he looked up at the corner where the wall met the ceiling. He almost fainted the first time he used the office, and he finally made it tolerable by filling it with plants to hide the room's shape. Chomsky also said that it was hard for him to do his work in this office because he could not hang a blackboard on a leaning wall.[47]

Though they have no deliberate symbolic content, Gehry's buildings inadvertently symbolize the fact that our society is devoted to sensationalism and to novelty, no matter what the expense in human terms.

Avant Gardists at Work

Daniel Libeskind might be the second most famous of the avant-gardist architects. His extension of the Denver Art Museum (Figure 5-6) has tilted walls and ceilings, which form sharp angles jutting out in many directions, and much of it is clad in titanium, like Gehry's Guggenheim museum. The building is made up of twenty planes, and none is parallel or perpendicular to another.

Figure 5-6: Daniel Libeskind, Frederic C. Hamilton Building of the Denver Art Museum, 2006. Notice that the building and the sculpture in front of it are in similar styles. You could design an avant-gardist building the same shape as the sculpture or an avant-gardist sculpture the same shape as the building.
Photo by Trueshow111.

When it opened, Christopher Hawthorne, architecture critic for the Los Angeles Times, said that the building made him dizzy and wrote "It's a really stunning piece of architectural sculpture," but the "aggressive forms" make it "a pretty terrible place for showing and looking at art."[48] Likewise, a local artist wrote a letter to the Denver Post saying that the sloping walls of the galleries made him physically sick: "After less than two minutes ... I had to leave. Art is visual, and the visual disorientation of the walls made me so nauseated and dizzy I could not enjoy the fabulous art, no matter how hard I tried." The director of the museum responded to this letter and did not deny that the building caused feelings of vertigo; instead, he said "Those are what great architectural spaces do to you."[49]

We have seen a few examples of the disorienting buildings the avant gardists design, and now we will look at an example of the bleak public spaces they design. When the Pritzker-Prize-winning architect, Thom Mayne, designed the new Federal Building in San Francisco, all the talk was about the "strikingly original" architecture silhouetted on the skyline, but in reality, the most striking thing about this building is the bleakness of its public space (Figure 5-7). When there is even a light breeze, this corner is filled with a whirlwind of dust, newspapers, and plastic bags. This is one case where a video would be better than a photo, because the photo gives you some idea of how dusty the space is but does not show how the wind blows the dust and trash around in circles.

A few years after the building opened, the local newspaper reported that this space had become a magnet for the homeless. The initial promotional material for the building said that it was "offering much-needed open space and services to the local community." But a local community resident says something very different about this space: "What you see there all day, 24/7, is people drinking, you see people urinating on the walls, you see everything." When you design this sort of bleak space, it is not surprising that the only people who are attracted

Figure 5-7: Thom Mayne, San Francisco Federal Building, 2007. A strikingly original way to create a bleak, unloved urban place. Photo by Charles Siegel.

to it are those who have no better choice. It is no more surprising to find homeless people here than to find them camping under a freeway overpass. The only thing that is surprising is that anyone ever took seriously the architect's claim that this space would become a hub for improving the neighborhood; apparently, they believed in the Pritzker Prize rather than believing their own eyes.

We have looked at examples of the starchitects' most extreme work, which disorients and even sickens the buildings' users. We should add that most of the starchitects' buildings just add artsy veneers to more-or-less conventional buildings. For example, Norman Foster's "Gherkin" in London (Figure 5-8) feels pretty much like any modern office building to the people who work in it. The building is just as sterile, impersonal and overwhelming as the boxy office buildings of the 1960s, but the artsy design has made it more acceptable to build corporate offices that damage London's traditional human scale. Far from being "subversive" rebels, starchitects are defenders of the corporate status quo.

A Parable

It would be monotonous to keep describing the foibles of our celebrity avant-gardist architects. They all have the same goal—being new and different, even if the building is uncomfortable and disorienting to its users. They all design buildings as abstract sculptural objects and as intellectual games, rather than designing good places for people.

Figure 5-8: Norman Foster and Arup Group, 30 St Mary Axe, London, 2003 (known as "The Gherkin"). The artsy design helps to justify another impersonal blockbuster office building, which clashes with London's traditional human-scale urban fabric. Photo by Aurelien Guichard.

Instead of making these same points about each of the avant gardists, we can sum up their approach by looking at the story of one of Peter Eisenman's early commissions.

In the late 1960s, Eisenman was known for his fiercely polemical and hard-to-read architectural manifestos, but he had only built one project, an addition to a house in Princeton that he called House I. He met Richard and Florence Falk at a cocktail party in Princeton, and they were so fascinated by his dense architectural theorizing that they hired him to design a house on a farm that they had purchased in Vermont, which he called House II. Richard Falk recalled in a later interview that, when Eisenman talked to him about a Chomskyesque house, "I don't know what it meant, but it sounded good."

When the Falks returned to their Vermont farm after a sabbatical, they found a house that was not yet complete but that would obviously be totally unusable. It had a flat roof, which was not practical in Vermont's heavy snow. It had a series of openings in the upper floors, which were meant to let light penetrate but which were also dangerous for the Falk's one-year-old son. It had hardly any interior walls: there were just half walls between the bedrooms. Because there were not complete walls, even a whisper could be heard through the entire house, and the Falk's son was not able to play inside during his entire childhood because his parents needed quiet to work.

The Falks were able to make the house usable by doing a major remodeling that included adding walls. Ms. Falk commented that Eisenman's design "was all about space, the eye moving with nothing to stop it" — which meant, she added, that it impressed visitors but was very hard to live in.

Three decades later, Eisenman responded to the Falk's criticisms of his house: "I don't design houses with the nuclear family idea because I don't believe in it as a concept. I was interested in doing architecture, not in solving the Falks' privacy problems."[50] When Eisenman talks about "doing architecture," he obviously means designing buildings for the cognoscenti who are interested in abstract art and obscure theoretical issues. He does not mean designing buildings that are good places for the people who use them.

A parable can help us understand why starchitecture is so inhuman. Once upon a time, there was a tailor who became famous by writing hard-to-read essays about sartorial theory, though he had never actually made any clothing except one suit for himself. Finally, his fame attracted a customer, and the tailor created a suit that was in keeping with his deconstructivist theory of clothing design. When the customer put on the suit, he found that it had an arm where the left leg should be, which made it painful to walk; it had a leg where the right arm should be, which made it difficult to use his right hand; and it had two arms coming out of random locations in the back of the suit jacket. The avant-gardist critics all said the design was brilliantly subversive of conventional ideas about what a suit should be. When the customer had the suit altered so he could walk around without pain, the tailor was furious and said, "I was interested in doing clothing design, not in solving his mobility problems."

At the end of the parable, we learn that this tailor obviously attracted very few customers and could not support himself designing such of uncomfortable clothing. He was forced to change his occupation, and he ended up doing honest work by getting a job as a taxi driver.

The difference is that tailors sell suits to the people who wear them, while architects often sell buildings to people who rarely use them. In particular, the trustees of museums and other cultural institutions enter the buildings only on occasion, and they do not have to live with the buildings' avant-gardist designs. Museum trustees also tend to have more money than knowledge, so they are easily impressed by the obscure theories of avant-gardist critics. The staffs of these cultural institutions do have to live with the buildings, but they tend to be so artsy that they are among the few who are eager to suffer in a building acclaimed by the critics.

This is why so many of our famous avant-gardist buildings are museums and other institutions dedicated to what now passes as high culture.

A Throwback

The *New York Times*' former architecture critic, Nicolai Ouroussoff, inadvertently admitted that his avant-gardism is a throwback when the *Times* called him back to write an obituary for Oscar Niemeyer.

Ouroussoff was notorious, when he was *New York Times* architecture critic, for focusing most of his articles on a small number of avant-gardist starchitects. He was the leading advocate of this style.

Niemeyer was notorious for his work on Brasilia (Figure 5-9), the new capital city that Brazil built between 1956 and 1960. Lucio Costa did the general plan, after winning a competition in 1956, and Niemeyer was the chief architect and designed the government buildings. Niemeyer had worked with Le Corbusier on the United Nations headquarters, and he said he was influenced by Le Corbusier. This influence is very obvious in Brasilia, and you can see in the illustration that Brasilia makes all the errors that have made today's city planners reject modernism. Wide arterial streets separate the government buildings in the center from the housing next to it, like a textbook example of how to make cities that do not work for pedestrians. The housing is in rows of identical high-rise slabs, like a textbook example of how to create sterile, lifeless housing projects. The government buildings face a large park-like space that is empty and devoid of life.

The city is designed as a work of abstract art rather than as a good place for people to live, and Ouroussoff loves that artsy design. He says of Niemeyer's government buildings, "His curvaceous, lyrical, hedonistic forms helped shape a distinct national architecture and a modern identity for Brazil." If you were a hedonist, would you want to live here? Ouroussoff is speaking as a disembodied esthete who enjoys contemplating Brasilia's design from a distance, and he does not care about what it is like to live there.

Most astounding, Ouroussoff admits in this article that his own view is actually a throwback to the modernism of the 1950s.

A decade or two after it was built, Brasilia was known as a model of everything that is wrong with modernist design. As Ouroussoff says:

> Modernism was by then falling out of favor with the architectural establishment. Brasília soon became a symbol of Modernism's failure to deliver on its utopian promises. The vast empty plazas seemed to sum up the social alienation of modern society; surrounded by slums, the monumental government buildings of its center exemplified Brazil's deeply rooted social inequalities.[51]

But beginning in the 1980s, the avant gardists whom Ouroussoff loves began to admire Brasilia again, as he says:

Figure 5-9: Oscar Niemeyer, principal architect, and Lucio Costa, principal planner, Brasilia, 1956-60. If you were a hedonist, would you rather live here or in Paris? Photo by Heitor Carvalho Jorge.

> ... a growing number of people had begun to re-examine the legacy of postwar Modernism and appreciate his [Niemeyer's] purist vision as a throwback to a more optimistic time.

Though he considers himself progressive, Ouroussoff actually admitted, at this unguarded moment, that people who think like him are throwbacks, nostalgic for the technological optimism of mid-century.

But we are not going to solve the problems of the twenty-first century by reviving the technophilia of the 1950s. Today, we have reached the point where we need to limit destructive effects of technology, rather than blinding ourselves to them. For example, city planners today recognize that we need a walkable street grid to connect business districts with nearby housing, in order to conserve energy and reduce greenhouse gas emissions. Ouroussoff ignores this point completely: he is nostalgic for an automobile-oriented 1950s design.

No serious urbanist would admire Brasilia, because urbanists have learned from the failures of modernism. But avant gardists have begun to admire Brasilia again, because they are reactionaries who want to revive the spirit of mid-century modernism.

Ouroussoff showed his reactionary bent even more clearly in an earlier column, written just after the death of Jane Jacobs, where he criticized her because "she never understood cities like Los Angeles, whose beauty stems from the heroic scale of its freeways ...."[52] It is hard to believe that he could criticize Jane Jacobs for appreciating walkable cities rather than freeway-oriented cities at a time when global warming had already begun and when the automobile was the largest source of greenhouse gases in California. They know better in Los Angeles itself: when Ouroussoff wrote this, Mayor Villaraigosa was supporting smart growth, with dense housing around transit stations, to change Los Angeles from a freeway-oriented to a pedestrian and transit-oriented city, and just two years later, California passed SB375 requiring that all of its cities plan for smart growth to help control global warming.

When Ouroussoff talks about the beauty of cities built around freeways, this spokesman for the avant gardists shows that he does not have a clue about the political issues that are important to progressives today.

He thinks of cities as aesthetic objects, and he looks down his nose at anyone who doesn't share his cliquish taste for the "beauty" of cities built around freeways — but his aesthetic is so retrograde that he does not have anything to be snobbish about. He wants to move backward in history — to ignore global warming, to ignore smart growth, to ignore the freeway revolts of the 1960s, and to go back to the "technological optimism" of Robert Moses and Sigfried Giedion. His comment about the "heroic scale" of the freeway echoes Giedion's talk about the "great scale" of the freeway.

This sort of thinking was understandable when Giedion wrote in 1941, but today we have had much more experience with urban freeways, and we know much more about global warming. When we hear someone who still advocates this sort of mid-century urbanism, we can only roll our eyes and think "how can anyone be so reactionary?"

Chapter 6
Architecture and Culture

So far, we have looked at features that are common to traditional architecture and urbanism across cultures because they are consonant with human nature. We used evolutionary psychology to explain the origin of some of these features. We saw that modernists abandoned them in favor of design focusing on new technologies and that when the failures of modernism became apparent, there was a revival of the "timeless way of building." Though this revival continues in urban design, it has stalled in architecture since the reactionary avant gardists revived modernism.

In addition to these common features, each style of traditional architecture had its own unique features that expressed the values and the sensibility of its own culture.

The New Urbanist criticism of modernist urbanism and Christopher Alexander's criticism of modernist architecture emphasize the features that are common to traditional design in all cultures—and rightfully so: because these common features were forgotten by modernists, it is essential that we relearn them. But by emphasizing what is common to human nature, they downplay the particular architectural styles that are unique to each culture.

So far, this book focused on the common features of traditional design across cultures, but now it will focus on traditional styles that differ among cultures and on how they express (or fail to express) larger cultural meaning.

Honest and Dishonest Architecture

The main objection to reviving traditional human-scale architecture is the old modernist dogma that architecture should be an "honest expression" of modern materials and functions. In this view, traditional architecture has historical ornamentation pasted onto the functional structure, which makes it look ersatz.

Yet a glance at architectural history will show that modernists were wrong to say that a style looks honest only if it is an expression of materials and function. In reality, architecture looks dishonest when style is used purely for ornamentation, and it looks honest when style expresses its culture's ideals.

For example, Renaissance architecture used historical ornamentation based on classical models, but no one would say that it looked like it looked like something from a theme park at the time when it was built. This ornamentation looked honest because it was an expression of a larger cultural ideal of its time, the revival of classical civilization.

By contrast, the eclectic historical architecture that became popular during the nineteenth and early twentieth centuries was designed to be picturesque. It looks dishonest because it was not an expression of the real ideals of a rapidly industrializing society.

The Greeks and Romans

Even early Greek temples, such as the Parthenon, used applied historical ornamentation, though no one says they look dishonest. The triglyphs over the columns in the Doric order (Figure 6-1) were probably derived from the wooden slab attached to the end of the wooden beams of pre-classical temples to protect the beam-ends from rotting, and the stone guttae below each triglyph from the wooden pegs that kept this slab in place. When they started building temples in stone, the Greeks kept these historical details from wooden temples as ornaments, even though they no longer had their original structural purpose.

Figure 6-1: Triglyphs and Guttae in the Temple of Aphaia II, on the Greek island of Aigina, about 500 BC. Photo by J. M. Harrington.

The Romans made even greater use of historical elements as applied decoration. They continued building temples using columns, but they built other public buildings using arches, which were an important advance over post-and-lintel stone construction because they could span larger spaces. Yet they added columns to these arched buildings, though they no longer had any function. Virtually all their public buildings have columns and pilasters (flat representations of columns) pasted on in front of the arches.

For example, the Colosseum in Rome (Figure 6-2) is made of three levels of arches topped by a wall. These arches, built of concrete faced with brick, were a remarkable structural achievement. But the Colosseum also has half-columns of three different classical orders in front of the arches on its lower three levels and pilasters in front of the wall on top. Modernists would say that it is dishonest to use this sort of pasted-on historical ornamentation, but in reality, the half-columns and pilasters have an important cultural meaning: they symbolize Rome's position as the heir to classical civilization and the importance of these public buildings.

Figure 6-2: Colosseum, Rome, 80 AD: The structure is made of three levels of arches topped by a wall. Columns in three orders are placed in front of the arches, and pilasters are placed in front of the wall, as decoration with no structural function. Photo by David Iliff.

The Renaissance

Renaissance architects made extensive use of two types of pasted-on historical ornamentation: pilasters and aedicules (windows or niches framed with columns or pilasters on their sides and with a cornice and pediment above). The Romans had used both of these, and they became key features of Renaissance architecture (Figure 6-3).

Pilasters imitate classical columns, which were structural elements of ancient Greek architecture, but the pilasters of the Renaissance are pasted onto walls as ornaments.

Likewise, aedicules imitate structural elements of Greek architecture — the columns were structural supports and the cornice and pediment were the roofline of the Greek temple — but the aedicules around the windows of Renaissance buildings are just pasted-on ornaments with no function.

There are other structurally dishonest features of Renaissance architecture. For example, it often uses hidden

Figure 6-3: Michelangelo and others, Palazzo dei Senatori, Rome, 1592-98. The pilasters on the upper two stories of the facade and the aedicules around the windows are pasted-on historical ornamentation, but they do not seem dishonest, because they are an expression of the Renaissance revival of classical culture. Photo by Wikibob.

tie-rods to strengthen arches and vaults that were not strong enough in themselves to stand the outward thrusts: this sort of hidden support was used in the domes that are a keynote of Renaissance architecture.

Filippo Brunelleschi (1377-1446) studied and measured ancient Roman monuments during his visits to Rome, and they were his inspiration when he designed the first buildings in the style of the Renaissance. Leon Battista Alberti (1404-1472) wrote *Ten Books on Architecture*, which carefully described the classical orders, the traditional vocabulary that could be used for fresh architectural expressions.

Modernists would say that all of this historicism, and the pasted-on ornaments that came with it, are horribly dishonest, but Renaissance architecture does not look dishonest. It looks as if the architects believed in what they were doing, because the architecture was part of a larger cultural movement to revive classical learning and culture.

Humanist scholars, beginning with Petrarch, rediscovered the classics. Artists revived naturalism, inspired by classical sculpture. The Renaissance named the period that preceded it the "Middle Ages" to imply that it was a barren and backward period between the fall of Roman civilization and the rebirth of classical civilization in their own time. They called medieval architecture "Gothic" to imply that it was the architecture of the barbarian Goths who invaded Rome—which was untrue but was effective propaganda.

The revival of classical architecture looks honest because it was an important part of the larger revival of classical civilization.

The Stage-Set Styles

The classical vocabulary of the Renaissance continued to dominate western architecture for centuries, through the mannerist, baroque, and Georgian styles, with differences that expressed the values of their times. For example, the flamboyance of the baroque symbolized the power of the aristocracy and monarchy during the seventeenth century, while the restraint of the Georgian style represented the eighteenth century's belief in reason and moderation. Even the most dogmatic modernist would not claim that any of these styles looked like a theme park at the time when it was being built. These styles were natural expressions of the values of their cultures, whose literature and political theories were rooted in classical models as well as their architecture. These styles still look natural and unaffected to us today.

Through most of the history of architecture, people took historical styles for granted, and no one considered them dishonest. Historical styles first began to look dishonest during the romantic period, as their love of the picturesque led the romantics to design buildings that were essentially stage sets.

The romantics loved to read novels about distant times and far-away places, and they built architecture that

116   *Humanists versus Reactionary Avant Garde*

Figure 6-4: Horace Walpole, Strawberry Hill, Twickenham, 1749-1776. Horace Walpole's house was as exotic as the settings of his Gothic novels, but this sort of romantic design was a rarity at the time. Photo by Chiswick Chap.

had the same exotic feel to it. A famous early example was Strawberry Hill (Figure 6-4), an eighteenth century impression of a Gothic castle, built by Horace Walpole, who was also the author of the first Gothic novel. Strawberry Hill was so exotic that a constant stream of visitors came to see it, as people today go to see theme parks.

During the eighteenth century, this sort of exoticism was a rarity, but in the nineteenth century, it became common. For example, the Greek Revival style of the early nineteenth century turned the classical style itself into something exotic. Rather than using the living classical tradition of the Georgian style, it built more accurate reproductions of ancient Greek temples, meant to evoke the feelings that we have when we see a building thousands of years old (Figure 6-5). This was one of a long series of revival styles meant to evoke romantic feelings.

The romantics also loved to read poetry about untamed nature, and they built architecture that had a wild and picturesque feel to it. The Eastlake and Stick styles (Figure 6-6), two typical Victorian styles of the late nineteenth century, did not evoke distant times or places, but they were

Architecture and Culture

Figure 6-5: William Strickland, Second Bank of the United States, Philadelphia, 1819-24. The Greek revival used Doric columns with no base, a historically correct reproduction of Greek architecture, instead of the living classical tradition of the time. The classical style itself became a romantic evocation of distant times and places. Photo by Peter Clericuzio.

Figure 6-6: Herman C. Timm House, New Holstein, Wisconsin, this portion built in 1891. This house is an example of the Stick/Eastlake style, which was picturesque without using detailing taken from historical styles. Photo by Royalbroil.

picturesque because of their multiple rooflines and gables, their turrets with witch's cap tops, their bay windows, and their decorative ornamentation.

Despite its love of the picturesque and the romantic, the nineteenth century still took architecture seriously. For example, John Ruskin and others hoped that a Gothic revival would make industrial England into a more Christian society that valued the dignity of workers. There was a "battle of the styles" during the nineteenth century, debating whether Gothic or classical style was the most appropriate expression of the culture of the times.

By contrast, the early twentieth century no longer took historical styles seriously at all. It produced a spate of historical styles that were purely picturesque and quaint, such as the Norman, the Tudor, the Spanish Colonial, and (most extreme) the Storybook or Hansel and Gretel style (Figure 6-7). The idea of using any historical style began

Figure 6-7: W. R. Yelland, Normandy Village, Berkeley, 1928. The Storybook style, was popular in California when Hollywood was becoming the manufacturer of the nation's fantasies. This is architecture as a stage set, charming but not something you can take seriously. Photo by Charles Siegel

to seem dishonest, because there was a rapid succession of artificial picturesque styles during the nineteenth and early twentieth century.

These picturesque styles reflected an inner split within their society. In Victorian and early twentieth-century society, commercial values and faith in progress were the real ideals that motivated people during the workweek. But people tried to escape this harsh economy by moving from industrial cities to suburbs, where they could live in picturesque houses and worship in Gothic revival churches — architecture that tried to deny the fact that they were living in a modern industrial society.

Modernism: A Bygone Ideal

When the early modernists began to claim that all historical ornamentation was dishonest, they were reacting against the dishonest historicism of their time, which tried to escape from the realities of the contemporary society.

Modernism was so striking when it was first introduced, not because it was an honest expression of materials and functions, but because it was an honest expression of the ideals of its time — the belief in technology, progress and efficiency.

The icons of the modernist style, were a striking statement of the twentieth century's technophilia, but as we have seen, they were not really an honest use of modern materials. For example, Mies' Farnsworth house and Philip Johnson's glass house both used steel skeletons and glass walls, when it would have been cheaper to build with a wood frame and more functional to build with smaller windows.

Modernism seemed so strikingly honest because it said frankly that the culture of its time centered on technology and economic growth. It did not paste a sentimental façade on the motivating ideals of its time, as the historical styles of the nineteenth and early twentieth century had.

For example, in the twentieth century, schooling began to focus on training students in the skills needed by the modern economy. But in the early twentieth century, it was fashionable to build high schools with Gothic facades, imitating Oxford and Cambridge, as if the new mass high schools were still ivied towers where students pursued learning for its own sake. By contrast with this sentimental facade, it seemed strikingly honest when modernists started building schools of unornamented steel, glass and concrete, showing that the schools were becoming an extension of the technological economy.

Style Without Meaning

Today, our society has moved beyond modernism. The technophilia symbolized by modernist architecture was the real ideal of our society in the early to mid-twentieth century, when modernization was lifting the masses out of poverty. It is no longer the ideal of today's society, which needs to humanize technology and control its destructive side effects.

Today's avant-gardism is a dishonest style, because we use it purely for decorative effect, without believing in its larger meaning. During the early to mid twentieth century, modernism was part of a larger social movement: like modernist architecture, socialism and liberalism looked forward to a better life in a prosperous technological society. By contrast, today's avant gardists have nothing to do with the larger political movements of our time or with the ideals of our society.

Yet many of today's traditional architects also use historical styles dishonestly, for decorative effect, without any larger social meaning. Most traditional architects practicing today concentrate on building human-scale architecture, and they have developed architecture and urbanism that contrasts very favorably with the sterile modernism of the mid twentieth century. But most are not trying to develop an architectural style that helps create meaning for the culture of our time.

There seem to be two main branches of traditional architecture today.

The break-up-the-box style is frank about giving up the search for larger meaning. It tries to create traditional, human-scale forms, but it does not try to add detailing that symbolizes cultural meaning.

Eclectic traditionalism uses decorative details from a variety of historical styles. The same architect might design buildings in classical style, Victorian style, streamlined moderne style, and also in a human-scale of the modernist style, showing that these styles are decorative and do not symbolize some larger cultural meaning that the architect believes in.

They sometimes use traditional styles with no conceivable meaning that is relevant to our time. For example, no one who designs in the streamlined moderne style today really means it, because we no longer have the naive fascination with streamlining that was common in the 1930s, when radios, clocks, and buildings in this style were all designed with the same streamlining as the latest locomotives, symbols of progress at the time.

Without realizing it, these eclectic architects have retained a bit of the ironic spirit of 1970s postmodernism. They do not deliberately mock traditional architecture, as Charles Moore did in Piazza d'Italia, but they are not serious about traditional architectural styles: they put on different styles in the way that you would put on costumes.

Historically, as we have seen, architectural styles have seemed honest when they reflected the ideals of their time, and they began to seem dishonest when they were used as picturesque stage sets. Our eclectics are using traditional styles purely to create a picturesque effect, as architects did in the early twentieth century.

Because these traditional architects do not take style seriously, their architecture has not become part of the larger cultural conversation of our time. Imagine if architects who actually did help to change their cultures had been like today's eclectics! If Alberti had said "As long as the buildings do a good job of defining piazzas and streets, I don't care if the decorations are classical or Gothic," he would not have helped to create the Renaissance. If Mies van der Rohe had said "As long as the buildings are towers in a park, I don't care if the decorations are steel I-beams or classical columns," he would not have helped to create the twentieth century's technological society.

Chapter 7
A Style for our Time

The history of architecture shows that traditional styles can be meaningful if the culture believes in what the style symbolizes. Today, there are some traditional architects who take style seriously, but most styles—both the traditional revival styles of the eclectics and the modernist revival style of the avant gardists—look a bit like they belong in a theme park, because the architects and the larger culture do not believe in what the styles symbolize. A meaningful architecture must be part of a larger cultural project.

My own opinion is that, as we move beyond the early period of modernization, we need a broad revival of classical western values. In my book, *Ethics: What We Still Know After a Skeptical Age*, I argue for classical Aristotelian ethics based on human flourishing. In my book, *The Politics of Simple Living*, I argue that we need to change the direction of our economy to promote human flourishing and quality of life, rather than promoting the highest possible rate of growth.

It is important to note that these classical values are not at all the same as the traditional values that conservatives support. In my book, *Classical Liberalism*, I show that this classical ideal of human flourishing was an important part of the American liberal tradition, beginning with Jefferson, and that it was central to the thinking of the abolitionist, feminist, and civil rights movements, which demanded that we reject traditional values that prevent some groups of people from flourishing and from developing their humanity fully. Classical liberalism is more relevant than ever today: during the industrial revolution, classical values were pushed aside to pave the way for growth of the modern economy, but now we need to revive values based on human flourishing to make good use of the modern economy.

Architecture could help bring about this revival of classical humanism today, as it did during the Renaissance.

Classicism for Our Time

Because it has been so important to western history, the classical vocabulary has been used to express the very different ideals of different times: Louis XIV used it to represent the grandeur of his absolute monarchy, and Thomas Jefferson used it to symbolize the virtues of the American republic. We can move beyond the eclecticism of today's traditional architecture by developing a classical style that expresses the emerging ideals of our time.

Modernist architecture expressed the technocratic ideal of a time when it was imperative to unleash the modern economy in order to overcome scarcity. Today, we need to subject the modern economy to human control, to use technology when it is beneficial and to limit technology when it damages the quality of life. If we think about the ways that our culture must change to tame the modern economy, we can sketch some features of a classical style for our time.

Simplicity

To counter the consumerism that is typical of the modern economy, we need an architecture that is restrained.

We should not imitate the indulgences of the baroque style or of the more ornate buildings in the Georgian style. Instead, we should be inspired by the simplicity and restraint of vernacular classical styles.

The ideal of simpler living—of a standard of living that lets us live a good life but does not embrace consumerism for its own sake—is essential to create a society that is sustainable environmentally.

New Urbanists have taken a big step in this direction by promoting urban design that allows simpler living, with houses on smaller lots in neighborhoods where you can walk rather than having to drive. We also need an architectural style that symbolizes restraint and simpler living.

Decentralization

To counter the excessive centralization and top-down control that is typical of the modern economy, we need an architecture that symbolizes pluralism—a society where decisions are made by many different people, not by one central authority.

We should not imitate the baroque and classical style of city planning that we see at St. Peters and Versailles, where one building dominates the symmetrical space around it to symbolize the power of a central authority. We should not imitate the beaux-arts city beautiful movement of a century ago, where one civic building dominates the symmetrical space around it.

Instead, we should be inspired by the informal layout of the Italian cities of the Renaissance (Figure 7-1), which were not centralized empires and still had republican ideals. We should also be inspired by the informal layout of ancient Rome, much of it developed under the republic, and by the informal streetscapes of the Georgian and Federal row house neighborhoods for the middle class.

The design by Leon Krier and Gabriele Tagliaventi for Borgo Città Nuova (1995-2002) in Alessandria, Italy, is a good example of this sort of informal classical design, which expresses the independence of each building and institution.

Human Scale

To counter the impersonality of the modern economy, we need an architecture that is human scale.

This is not just a matter of density. High-rise developments are impersonal, but low-density suburban strip malls are also impersonal.

We need to build walkable neighborhoods with local

Figure 7-1: Leon Krier and Gabriele Tagliaventi, Borgo Città Nuova (1995-2002). The informal classical design symbolizes pluralism, the independence of each building and institution. Photo by Civicarch

shopping, as the New Urbanists have already begun to do. They can be the density of traditional European cities that have four to six-story apartment buildings, or the density of streetcar suburbs that have three- to five-story Main Streets within walking distance of single-family homes. Ideally, these neighborhoods should be built by small developers of individual houses and apartment buildings, not by one developer who builds an entire neighborhood.

We also need human-scale architectural style: instead of the flat, featureless, impersonal surfaces of modernist buildings, we need decorative elements to break up surfaces into subsections that are human-scale.

Historic Continuity

To counter the modern economy's tendency to discard the past, we need an architectural style that symbolizes historic continuity.

The modernists wanted to reject past styles completely and invent a totally new, rational style of architecture, just as they wanted to tear down existing neighborhoods completely and replace them with rationally planned housing projects. They saw this discontinuity as a source of hope: they were rejecting the past in order to build a better technological future.

Today, we see this sort of discontinuity as a threat. We have learned that modernist urban renewal destroys functioning communities. We know that global warming threatens to disrupt nature drastically.

To symbolize historical continuity in western Europe and the United States, we must use a classical vocabulary, the closest thing we have to a continuous style, running from the Greeks, to the Romans, the Renaissance, the Baroque, the Georgian, and the Greek revival, Renaissance revival, Beaux Arts, Roman Renaissance, and Colonial Revival styles of the nineteenth and twentieth centuries.

Of course, we must accommodate change as well as continuity, in order to take advantage of new technologies. Some of our great classical buildings have used new technologies to create something different from any past building. For example, McKim, Mead, and White's Municipal Building (Figure 7-2) in downtown Manhattan was designed after the steel skeleton and elevator made it possible to build taller buildings, and after the expansion of city government made it necessary to build an office building to hold a large bureaucracy; but this building's classical detailing says that, even as it uses new technologies, it does not break with the civic ideals of the past.

Local Styles

To counter the globalization typical of the modern economy, which is imposing the same standardized corporate culture on the entire world, we need to create local classical styles.

These styles should be adapted to the local climate and should use local materials. The modernists thought that

128 *Humanists versus Reactionary Avant Garde*

Figure 7-2: McKim, Mead, and White, Municipal Building, New York, 1907-14. The building's classical detailing symbolizes continuity of civic values, even though it makes use of new technologies such as the steel skeleton to create a type of building that never existed in the past. Photo by Charles Siegel.

heating and air conditioning technology would let us build the same glass boxes everywhere, but now we know that energy supplies are limited and that buildings should be designed to reduce the burden of heating and cooling.

Local styles also symbolize historical continuity. The architectural style that creates a sense of continuity with the past is obviously different in England and in Italy, for example.

Finally, local styles symbolize independent local cultures—just the opposite of the modernists' international style, which symbolized global technocracy.

Culture Over Technology

To counter the modern economy's tendency to make decisions on a purely technical basis, ignoring human values, we need to create a style that symbolizes the dominance of culture over technology.

The modernist style symbolized the autonomy of technology: design was supposed to be a pure expression of a building's materials and function.

If a classical style expresses all the values that we have already looked at, it would also symbolize the dominance of culture over technology: technology is not autonomous but is used in a way that reflects the culture.

Local Classical Styles

Though eclectics are in the majority, a number of today's traditional architects are serious classicists. Eclectics sometimes accuse the classicists of being narrow-minded and rigidly following rules laid down in the past; in reality, most of them see classicism as a living tradition that is changing as it deals with the challenges of the present. The classicists' forms are human scale, and their style is in the mainstream of the western tradition. There are classicists today who mean what they are saying, so their buildings do not look like stage sets.

These architects have begun to develop a new style for our time. We will look at a few examples, which are not meant to be a survey of contemporary classicism but just an indication of the direction that we could be moving.

Classicism in Europe

It is relatively easy to develop a local classical style in countries that have their own strong classical tradition, such as England and Italy.

A good example of a local classical style for England is Quinlan Terry's Richmond Riverside neighborhood in

Figure 7-3: Quinlan Terry, Richmond Riverside neighborhood, London, 1984-1987. This project is in the style of a traditional London neighborhood, and it does not look artificial at all. These classical buildings look like they belong right where they are, but glass boxes would be out of place here. Photo by David Iliff.

London (Figure 7-3). Terry often points out that this sort of traditional construction using local materials is more environmentally sound than modernist construction, because it needs less heating and cooling and because it lasts for centuries. This development also shows that traditional neighborhoods can be built at a reasonable cost. Unfortunately, Terry has generally worked on individual homes and has not had many opportunities to build this sort of major project because of the current prejudice against classical architects.

A good example of a classical style for Italy is David Mayernik's design for the campus of the American school in Lugano, Switzerland. The planned campus is simple and restrained, with relatively little ornamentation. Though individual buildings are symmetrical, the design as a whole is informal and asymmetrical. It is human scale. It expresses continuity with the past and with local styles: the school is

A Style for our Time

Figure 7-4: David Mayernik, Exterior of the Fleming Library of American School, Lugano, Switzerland, 1996. This new architecture is in keeping with the traditional classical style of its location. Photo by Roberto Paltrinieri.

Figure 7-5: David Mayernik, Interior of the Fleming Library at the American School. This simply looks like a normal library interior, showing that today's classicism can be a natural and unaffected style. Photo by Roberto Paltrinieri.

in the Italian-speaking portion of Switzerland, and it fits into its context perfectly.

The interior of the Fleming Library (Figures 7-4 and 7-5), one of the buildings on this campus that has already been completed, shows very clearly that classicism can be a natural and unaffected style. This is not a stage-set style meant to look picturesque. It simply looks like a library interior should look, and people in the library may not even notice the classical vocabulary.

There are many other examples in Europe of local traditional styles that look natural and unaffected, such as Demetri Porphyrios' Pitiousa in Spetses; Francois Spoerry's Coeur de Ville of Le Plessis-Robinson outside of Paris; Maurice Culot and Caroline Mierop's Rue de Laeken in Bruxelles; and Jose Cornelio da Silva's work in Portugal.

Classicism in The United States

It is harder to develop a local neo-classical style in much of the United States, particularly in the West.

In the East, the vernacular classical homes of the early nineteenth century and the classical revival styles provide a link to the main classical tradition. For example, the New Urbanist town of I'On Mount Pleasant, South Carolina (Figure 7-6), has many homes in the traditional classical style of the southeastern United States, with deep porches for shade.

But in the western United States, whose history does not go back as far, architecture is dominated by the picturesque styles and by modernism. These places do have one common historical style that is an excellent basis for a new classicism, sometimes called the "classical box" (Figure 7-7).

This style was popular among home builders in much of America near the beginning of the twentieth century. The boxy building is varied with simplified classical columns around the front entrance, with one or two bay windows, and with a hip roof. Many houses in this style have some additional ornamentation, such as classical pilasters at the four corners of the house, or dentils at the roofline.

A Style for our Time 133

Figure 7-6: Homes at I'On, Mount Pleasant, South Carolina, town design by Dover, Kohl and Duany Plater-Zyberk, Town founded in 1995. The town has many homes in the traditional classical style of the southeastern United States.

Figure 7-7: A Vernacular Edwardian Classical Box, c. 1905—1910. The classical ornamentation and the massing give this style a feeling of stability, restraint, and continuity with the past. Without the bit of historical ornamentation, the house would just be a box. Photo by Charles Siegel.

This ornamented box is obviously less expensive to build than the houses with broken-up massing and multiple gables that today's builders often use to give their homes some character. Ironically, the modernists rejected ornamentation in the name of efficiency, but now home builders go through so many contortions to break up the boring modernist box that they build in ways that are inefficient. A classical box with a bit of pasted on historical ornamentation would be a more efficient design, and its proportions and classical detailing could give it real architectural character.

Our goal should be to create a classical style for fabric buildings that seems as unaffected today as the classical box, Georgian row house, and other classical vernaculars seemed in their time. The classical detailing is so central to our architectural tradition that people could begin to take it for granted again, as they did a century ago.

Important public buildings demand stronger design than these fabric buildings. A good example that would work in most of the United States is David Schwartz's Schermerhorn Symphony Center in Nashville (Figure 7-8), whose appearance is reminiscent of museums and symphony halls built a century ago.

Though it is in classical style, Schermerhorn Symphony Center is very innovative technologically. It is the first symphony hall that has a motorized system to shift from the raked seating used during symphonies to a flat floor used during other events. It has acoustical panels that can be adjusted by pushing a button to fine-tune the concert hall's acoustics for amplified music or symphony performances. It has a TV system that lets latecomers see and hear the performance until there is a break that allows them to take their seats. To block external noise, it has a double concrete envelope and an acoustical isolation joint around the concert hall.[53]

In addition to being a good example of classical design, this building is a good example of a sensible attitude toward modernization. It uses the latest technology when it actually

A Style for our Time

Figure 7-8: David Schwartz's Schermerhorn Symphony Center, Nashville, 2006.
This building is reminiscent of museums and symphony halls built a century ago.
Photo by Kerry Woo.

is useful to enhance the experience of concertgoers. But it is not like avant-gardist buildings, whose design is based on showing off new technology, even if it makes the buildings dysfunctional for its users.

Classicism Outside the West

In most of Western Europe and the United States, we can symbolize historical continuity only by using a classical vocabulary. In other parts of the world, we would expect architects to use their own traditional styles to symbolize continuity — but we would also expect them to come to grips with their cultures' encounter with the West.

When Peter the Great decided to westernize Russia, he built a new capital for the country in the classical style, St. Petersburg. He also forcibly cut off the beards of the men in his court, imitating western style. The debate about architecture was a debate about culture, and Slavophiles loved buildings with onion domes just as stubbornly as Peter loved buildings with classical columns.

Today, much of the world is adopting some western values, such as democracy, human rights, and freedom of speech, and these values seem to be a real advance. Perhaps the ideal is a synthesis of each culture's traditional values with these classical western values — and if we took architecture as seriously as Peter the Great and the Slavophiles did, this would also involve a synthesis of the culture's traditional architecture with classical architecture. Of course, each culture must decide this for itself, and we would expect conflicts among traditionalists and westernizers along the way.

Modernists sometimes say that the classical style is a symbol of nineteenth-century European imperialism, but there is nothing imperialistic about saying that each culture should use historic architectural styles as part of its own attempt to make sense of its history and of its future.

On the contrary, the real symbol of imperialism today is the modernist style — which was invented in the west, which claims to be valid everywhere, and which is being imposed on the world by multinational corporations.

Reconstructing Our Culture

This chapter has sketched some features of a classical architectural style that would express the cultural values needed in our time: simplicity to counter the economy's tendency toward consumerism, pluralism to counter the tendency toward top-down control, human scale to counter the tendency toward impersonality, historic continuity to counter the tendency to throw away the past, local styles to counter the tendency toward globalization znc the dominance of culture over technology to counter the tendency to make decisions on technical grounds rather than on a human grounds.

A Style for our Time

I, myself, believe that a revival of classical humanism could help subordinate technology to human values. Just as the Renaissance saw the Middle Ages as an interruption in the development of western civilization, I think that we need to see that the industrial revolution has been an interruption to the development of western civilization, because it focused on technological values rather than on humanistic values. This focus was beneficial at the time, because it cleared the way for the economic growth needed to eliminate scarcity, but now we must move beyond it. I believe that a revival of classical architecture should be part of a broader cultural change that also includes the revival of the classical moral philosophy of human flourishing and the classical liberal politics that I have written about in other books.

Others will disagree and believe that we need a different architectural style—and a different direction for our culture. A fruitful debate can begin when we all see that creating a vital architectural style is not just a question of how to decorate our buildings but that it is also part of a larger cultural project.

There are some obvious historical examples showing that architecture can attempt to transform the culture in this way, sometimes successfully and sometimes not.

The Renaissance style of architecture was one part of the larger revival of classical culture at the time, which was immensely successful and has influenced western culture ever since.

The Gothic revival of the nineteenth century, inspired by the writing of John Ruskin, was initially part of an attempt to change society by rejecting industrialization and reviving a crafts economy. This larger cultural project did not succeed, because it was unrealistic to expect to replace factories with much less productive handicrafts. As a result, the Gothic became another decorative style.

The shingle style (Figure 7-9) was a more modest attempt to change society by replacing Victorian formality with a more informal way of living and also by reviving

Figure 7-9: Edgar Fisher Soulé, Anna Head School, Berkeley, 1892. The shingle style rejected Victorian formality in favor of a more informal way of living. Imagine how it felt a century ago to see this school building instead of the usual Gothic or neoclassical school buildings of this time. Photo by Charles Siegel

craftsmanship. Architecture did lead the way in making society less formal: decades after they built those homes without Victorian ornamentation, people began to wear casual clothing rather than suits and ties, to call each other by their first names, and so on. The attempt to revive craftsmanship was less successful because it is unrealistic to replace industrial methods with crafts.

The modernist style of the early to mid-twentieth century was part of a change to a more technological society. It was very successful and is a powerful example of how architecture can advocate for larger social changes.

I don't expect everyone to agree with me that our time needs a classical revival, but I do hope that architects will begin to think about the larger cultural implications of their work and try to develop styles that reflect the social changes needed in our time. A good first step would be a new "battle of the styles," like the debate among nineteenth century architects and critics about whether the classical or gothic style symbolizes the best direction for society.

Yet most traditional architects today are not engaged with these larger cultural and political issues. Most neo-traditional architecture is a statement against modernist esthetics, but not a statement about the direction that our culture should take. Robert A.M. Stern, the most important historian of the neo-traditional movement, says explicitly that it is not engaged with moral or political issues:

> In Modern Traditionalism, ... the moral issues of architecture are left to the political or ideological, rather than the structural, realm. The result is that ... Modern traditionalism has many of the qualities of the eclecticism that enlivened nineteenth- and early twentieth-century architecture.[54]

This decorative eclecticism is exactly what the modernists rejected. This amoral and apolitical stance prevents us from developing a coherent new style to replace modernism.

Architecture cannot succeed — even in esthetic terms — if it only deals with esthetic issues and refuses to engage the larger cultural issues of its time. As long as most of our neo-traditional architects use traditional styles as decoration, rather than trying to express an ideal for our time, much of their work will continue to look inauthentic, and modernists will continue to say that it looks like it belongs in a theme park.

Chapter 8
A Meaningful Skyline

Most of the basic principles of the New Urbanism are now widely accepted by city planners, such as using a street grid with buildings oriented toward the sidewalk and locating a variety of uses within walkable distance of each other, but high-rises remain a source of controversy among city planners—including New Urbanists.

Many city planners support high-rises because they believe in smart growth, which calls for higher densities to make cities more walkable and to conserve open space. If higher densities are good, their reasoning seems to go, than high-rises must be even better.

Yet many others make the obvious point that the high-rises seem faceless and impersonal. If our goal is to build human-scale cities as part of a larger project of humanizing our technological society, then we should reject high-rises in favor of the mid-rise scale of traditional European neighborhoods.

Limiting Heights

The famous Danish urbanist, Jan Gehl, provides a good explanation of why high-rises seem impersonal in his book *Life Between Buildings*, which is probably the best book available about designing lively urban places. In a series of views, Gehl shows that people in the street and in a building's second and fifth floors can see each other clearly, but there is barely visual contact from the eighth floor, and none at all from the sixteenth floor. Gehl says:

> Meaningful visual contact with ground level events is possible only from the first few floors in a multi-story building. Between the third and forth floor, a marked decrease in the ability to have contact with the ground level can be observed. Another threshold exists between the fifth and sixth floors. Anything and anyone above the fifth floor is definitely out of touch with ground level events.[55]

Thus, the people who live on most of the floors in high-rises have no visual connection with the street from their apartments.

When you walk through a traditional urban neighborhood, with buildings five or six stories high, you can see personalizing details such as flowerpots in windows, and you can sometimes see the faces of people looking out of their windows. When you walk through a high-rise neighborhood, you can see these personalizing details in the lower floors, but the upper floors lack these visible details and have all the humanity of a piece of graph paper.

I would not make the fifth floor the cutoff height, as Gehl does. The traditional neighborhoods of Paris certainly do not seem impersonal, though they often have fabric buildings of seven or eight stories. But above the eighth floor or so, people living in a high rise have no visual connection with the surrounding community; they just look out at a distant view, unless that view is blocked by another high rise. The residents of the buildings are cut off visually from the nearby streets, and the people walking in those streets are surrounded by faceless buildings.

High-rises are not necessary to get the density needed for smart growth. Paris, still dominated by its traditional neighborhoods despite some recent modernist additions, is more than four time the density of Vancouver, which is famous for its high-rises.[56] There are recent examples of neo-traditional neighborhoods with a height limit of five stories that have densities of over 60 people per acre, high enough density to achieve the goals of smart growth by eliminating auto-dependency and preserving open space from sprawl.[57]

If our goal is to create cities that are comfortable, human-scale places for people to live, we should create this traditional skyline, with midrise fabric buildings.

Rising Above the Urban Fabric

In addition to preserving the human scale, limiting heights can give us a meaningful skyline. As we have seen, New Urbanists point out that what they call "fabric buildings"—utilitarian buildings such as housing, office buildings and commercial buildings—should have consistency with variation. Form-based codes and design codes make the fabric buildings generally consistent and still let each building be designed individually.

But New Urbanists also say that important public buildings should be exempt from the codes, so they stand out from the fabric created by these utilitarian buildings. Though many New Urbanists would allow a high-rise fabric, this design principle clearly works best if fabric buildings have their height limited, so that important public buildings are visible on the skyline.

This is a common design principle in traditional cities and towns. In Vermont towns, for example, the fabric of the main street is made up of rows of two or three story buildings with storefronts facing the sidewalk, but the town hall is set back from the sidewalk with a lawn in front, and it rises above the fabric buildings. The residential streets are made up of two-story houses, but the churches in these neighborhoods rise above the fabric buildings. When you look at the town from a distance, there is a meaningful skyline, with the spires of the churches and the cupola of town hall rising above the urban fabric, symbolizing the activities that were most important to the people who built these towns.

A Meaningful Skyline

Figure 8-1: Haarlem, Netherlands. This city has a meaningful skyline that is typical of traditional European cities, with the medieval cathedral (which became a Protestant church during the reformation) rising above the fabric buildings, showing that religion was central to the meaning of its people's lives.
Photo by Charles Siegel.

Figure 8-2: Florence, Italy. Because medieval Florence was a republic, the city government was also central to its people's lives. The Palazzo Vecchio (the city hall with the bell tower, left) and the Duomo (the cathedral with dome and campanile, right) are the two most prominent buildings on its skyline
. Photo by Charles Siegel.

The same design principle applies in traditional European cities: ordinary buildings are five or six stories tall, and the cathedral and other important buildings rise above the fabric buildings, giving the city a meaningful skyline that symbolizes the activity that was most important to the people who built it (Figures 8-1 and 8-2).

This traditional design not only makes these places attractive esthetically. It also expresses the residents' civic and religious ideals—showing that these ideals are more important than their everyday activities.

This sort of skyline seems to contradict a principle developed in Chapter 2: thinking about the psychology of hunters and gatherers, we said that people are attracted by a consistent, varied urban fabric, but we did not say anything about larger buildings rising above the fabric—and of course, hunters and gatherers did not build these larger buildings. Yet people all over the world did start to build large structures with symbolic meaning soon after they began building permanent settlements, from the ziggurats of the Babylonians to the pyramids of the Aztecs.

Figure 8-3: Grave Creek Mound, Moundsville, West Virginia, about 250-150 BC. This mound, 62 feet high and 240 feet in diameter, was built by the Adena culture, which lived largely by hunting and gathering but also cultivated squash and sunflower. With the beginning of agriculture came monuments with symbolic value that rose above the culture's fabric buildings. Photo by Tim Kiser.

Less developed cultures also built cruder versions of these monumental structures, such as Stonehenge in England and the earthworks of the mound builders of the Mississippi and Ohio River valleys (Figure 8-3).

Apparently, people do have an evolved need for cultural meaning. They satisfy this need in hunter-gatherer societies through myth, song, and ritual. As soon as they begin to build permanent structures, they also satisfy this need with symbolic buildings and monuments.

American Skyline

Traditional cities and towns were built with this sort of symbolic skyline because ordinary construction techniques limited the scale of the fabric buildings. Extraordinary efforts were needed to construct buildings that rose above the fabric — cathedrals could take centuries to build — and people made these efforts only for the most important buildings.

Today's construction techniques make it easy to build high-rises, so we need laws imposing height limits to create the same sort of meaningful skyline.

Without height limits, we get the typical skyline of most American cities, dominated by high-rise office buildings. This skyline has unintentional symbolism: we let the corporate developers build what they want because economic growth is the central value of modern American culture, just as Christianity was the central value of medieval European culture.

Many planners admire Vancouver, where the city has encouraged development with three or four-story buildings facing the sidewalks, often with shopping on the first floor, and with high-rise towers in the center of the block. The facades facing the sidewalk create lively streets; the towers provide extra density, and because they are set back in the middle of the street, they do not block light and views.

The Vancouver model can create consistent but varied

Figure 8-4: The Vancouver Skyline. The Vancouver model can create street life at the ground level, but it creates a sterile, impersonal skyline rather than a meaningful skyline. Photo by Thom Quine,

fabric buildings, but it gives us a meaningless skyline—an endless procession of utilitarian high-rises, which give no sense at all of what people consider the central values of their lives (Figure 8-4). It gives us a skyline that looks very much like the skyline of Le Corbusier's Radiant City, though it gives us livelier streets at ground level. Planners who admire this model focus on a few simple goals—high density, stores facing the streets, light and views for each apartment—and ignore broader cultural issues.

Washington, DC, is the major American city with height limits for fabric buildings and with important public buildings and symbolic structures that stand out above the fabric. The Capitol dome and the Washington Monument dominate its skyline, symbolizing the civic values that the national capital is supposed to embody. Washington is proof that a contemporary city can have the same sort of meaningful and attractive skyline found in traditional cities.

Washington is a special case: because it is the seat of national government, the Capitol dome dominates the skyline. As a general rule we would have a much more pluralistic skyline if we built modern cities according to the design principle that the height of fabric buildings should be limited and important buildings should rise above the fabric. In the center of the city, civic buildings such as city hall, cultural institutions such as museums, and the major buildings of a number of religions could all rise above the utilitarian fabric buildings. In the neighborhoods, local civic buildings such as libraries and schools, and a variety of houses of worship could rise above the neighborhood's homes and businesses.

This sort of skyline would symbolize the belief that there are more important things to life than the economy—just the opposite of the high-rise skyline of the typical American city. This skyline would be a powerful symbol that society subordinates technology to human values.

When we try to visualize this imaginary city, it is hard for us to see exactly which buildings would rise above the fabric, because we do not know what the people living in the city consider most important. It is hard for us to see exactly what the style of its architecture is: it looks classical to me, but it undoubtedly looks different to others. Yet we can see clearly that the city has public buildings rising above the fabric and has a symbolically meaningful architectural style, both expressing the ideals of the people who live there.

Chapter 9
From Modernism to Humanism

This book has looked at why modernism is obsolete and at the sort of architecture needed to respond to the conditions of our time. Modernism made some sense in the early twentieth century, when we needed to unleash technology to overcome scarcity. It no longer makes sense today, when we need to deliberately use technology for human purposes. Because our economic situation has changed, we need to replace modernism with humanism — and modernist architecture with a meaningful humanistic architecture.

In the mid-twentieth century, modernists had a coherent theory about architecture, which they summed up in their slogan, "Form Follows Function." They no longer use this slogan, because most avant-gardist buildings today use technology for show rather than for function: there is nothing functional about a blob-shaped building coated with titanium. Now that we have abandoned the idea that architecture should be an expression of function, there is no longer any theoretical basis for rejecting historical styles.

Today's avant-gardists sometimes claim that their buildings are subversive. As we have seen, their deconstructivist theories are not worth much because they do not think about exactly what they are subverting, so they do not see that they are working against human nature. The jargon also has not caught on with the public, because it is so obscure.

The claims that have influenced the public are even weaker. The avant-gardists attack traditional styles by repeating clichéd catch phrases. Most misguided of all, the avant-gardists claim that traditional architecture is conservative and they are progressive.

We need to see that these emperors of architecture have no clothes, so we can get on with the real work of creating a humanistic architecture for our time.

Modernist Catch Phrases

Anyone who cares about architecture constantly runs into catch phrases that are used to dismiss traditional architecture. Any architecture that learns from earlier styles is "nostalgic," it looks like it belongs in a "theme park," and it is not "of our time."

These catch phrases get in the way of developing architecture that responds to the real needs of our time, so we should make it clear that their catch phrases are hollow.

Nostalgia

Before 1920, the word "nostalgia" referred to a medical condition found in soldiers who were so traumatized by battle that they had a pathological desire to return to home. The word was first used in 1920 in its current sense, to mean a generalized longing for the past. The current sense became popular because the modernist movement of that time needed the word.

If you look at the writing of that time, you will see that modernists were willing to use wildly utopian models of the future, but they criticized people who used any models from the past. The best-known futuristic model is the communist ideal of an industrial workers' utopia, a favorite of intellectuals of the early and mid-twentieth century. We have seen that city planners used equally extreme futuristic models, such as Le Corbusier's radiant city.

In reality, it is obviously best to choose on a case-by-case basis whether to use models from the past or from the future, thinking in each case about which model does the most to enhance our well-being—rather than automatically rejecting the past in favor of progress or automatically rejecting the future in favor of tradition. We should not let an empty catch phrase like "nostalgia" stop us from thinking about which model is best in any given case.

For example, New Urbanists have designed neighborhoods laid out like the old streetcar suburbs because they think it is better to live where you can walk to shopping and other services, rather than living in a sprawl suburb where you have to drive every time you leave home. But New Urbanist developments also use up-to-date heating, air-conditioning, and kitchen equipment, unlike the original streetcar suburbs, which used coal for cooking and heating and had no air conditioning.

They are not nostalgic for the days when the streetcar suburbs were built, when coal was the main fuel and when women did not have the right to vote. But they do see that we can learn some things from those days, if we think about them in enough detail to avoid what was bad but learn from what was good about them. They see that they can get the best result by learning how to build walkable neighborhoods from past models, and by using the most advanced technologies when they are appropriate.

Theme Park Architecture

Avant gardists often say that traditional architecture looks like a "theme park." They are right that today's traditional architecture sometimes looks artificial, when the architects are using traditional styles decoratively without really believing in them, but they do not notice that their own avant-gardist architecture also looks artificial, because they use futuristic styles decoratively without really believing in them.

They forget that the original Disneyland included "Tomorrowland" as well as "Main Street, USA."

The modernists chortled when Disney Corporation built Celebration, Florida—a New Urbanist town built by our most famous theme park-developer. But a few years later, we also got Walt Disney Concert Hall in downtown Los Angeles, a Frank Gehry building that looks like a shiny avant-gardist sculpture.

Which of these two is more like a theme park? By definition, a theme park is built to lure tourists with experiences that they cannot get elsewhere.

Celebration was designed as a Victorian town because that is the sort of place where its residents want to live. Its architecture is sentimental, but it was not designed to attract tourists like a theme park.

There is one architect today who is famous for his ability to attract tourists. When he built the Guggenheim museum in Bilbao, Spain, its bizarre design attracted so many gaping tourists that it revitalized the city's economy. After that success, cities all over the world wanted similar buildings to stimulate their economies by attracting tourists—and Los Angeles got him to design Walt Disney Concert Hall to revitalize its downtown by attracting those gaping tourists. There is no doubt that Frank Gehry is our most successful designer of theme park architecture—but many other avant gardists are trying hard to imitate him.

Sometimes our neo-traditional architecture looks something like a theme park, but our avant-gardist architecture looks even more like a theme park (Figure 9-1). Most of our traditional neighborhood developments are "historically themed," while most of our museums and cultural centers are "themed" in the avant-gardist style.

By contrast, some buildings inspired by classical styles do not seem to be "themed," because the classical vocabulary is so central to the history of western architecture, and because the architects believe in what they are doing. For example, the projects by Quinlan Terry and David Mayernik mentioned earlier do not look like theme park architecture. They simply look like they belong in London and in Italy. Likewise David Schwartz's Schermerhorn Symphony Center in Nashville does not look "themed": classicism is so engrained in our history that it simply looks like a civic building should look.

152 *Humanists versus Reactionary Avant Garde*

Figure 9-1: Theme Park Architecture. Of these two recent symphony halls, which one is designed to look like a symphony hall, and which one is designed to attract gaping tourists like a theme park? Above, David Schwartz, Schermerhorn Symphony Center in Nashville (2006). Photo by Kerry Woo. Below, Frank Gehry, Walt Disney Concert Hall in Los Angeles (2003). (Photograph by PDphoto.org.)

Architecture of Our Time

As another common catch phrase, avant gardists claim that only modernist architecture is "of our time." But this architecture does not respond to the needs of our time: the last thing we need in our time is to ignore human values and to adopt every flashy technology purely for the sake of being new and different.

The modernism of the early and mid-twentieth century really was of its time. This architecture was appropriate to a scarcity economy that needed new technology to bring prosperity. It was the appropriate architecture for a culture that wanted to throw away any limits to progress and to build its way out of every problem.

Since the 1970s, though, there has been a change in sensibility as our culture has moved beyond this sort of technophilia.

This change in sensibility has occurred in our attitude toward food. Imagine people saying that they eat mass produced white bread and McDonalds hamburgers because they are "of our time," while artisanal bread and food made from locally grown ingredients are just examples of "nostalgia" about how food used to be made. Everyone would see that they are wrong to think that we should decide what to eat based on which foods are modern, rather than on which foods are the healthy and tasty. And everyone would see that they are even more wrong to think this modernist approach to food is "of our time": it actually was common during the mid-twentieth century, but we have moved beyond it since the 1960s and 1970s.

This change of sensibility has occurred in city planning. Imagine people saying that they support building new freeways that slice through urban neighborhoods, because freeways are the transportation "of our time," while people who want walkable neighborhoods are just "nostalgic" for the way people used to get around. Everyone would see that they were wrong to decide what sort of cities to live in based on what is modern, rather than on what sort of neighborhood is most livable, convenient, healthy, and sustainable. And everyone would see that they were even more wrong to think that this modernist approach is "of our time": it actually was common during the mid-twentieth century, but we have moved beyond it since the 1960s and 1970s.

This change of sensibility has happened across the culture, but the architectural establishment has missed it. The change began to occur among serious postmodernist architects, but the reactionary avant garde rejected it. As in other fields, everyone should see that the architectural establishment is wrong to think we should decide how to design our buildings based on what is modern, rather than on how livable and how attractive the buildings are. And everyone should see that they are even more wrong that this modernist approach is "of our time," when it is actually a step backwards to the 1950s and beyond.

What is Progressive?

Avant gardists claim that, because their architecture is futuristic, it is politically progressive, while traditional architecture is politically conservative.

To make our architecture relevant to the key political questions of our time, we need to reject this idea. In today's technological society, the modernists support the status quo while the humanists are working for social change.

From Radical to Establishment

The avant-garde style began around the time of World War I, became generally accepted during mid-century, and has become the establishment style today—which is why it is now "avant gardist" rather than genuinely avant garde.

A century ago, its gestures seemed radical because they rejected the traditional society that dominated Europe and the United States. At that time, it made some sense to believe that radicalism involved a total break with the past.

During the 1950s, modernism still had some of its early

radical spirit. It was not only on the leading edge esthetically but also on the leading edge of progressive social reform. The freeways and the high-rise housing projects were still part of the progressive project of getting the masses out of the slums by providing suburban housing for the middle class and sanitary public housing for the poor. Glass-steel-and-concrete modernism was still an exciting break with the past, symbolizing the rejection of oppressive traditions.

During the 1960s, modernism became common enough that everyone saw it was failing. Modernist housing projects became vertical slums that were worse than the old slums they replaced. Freeways spread sprawl and blighted older neighborhoods. There were citizens' revolts against both of these modernist impositions on existing neighborhoods — and these movements represented a new direction for progressive politics.

During the 1970s, it became clear that modernism was now the status quo, and it was oppressive. The glass and steel office buildings towering over the old downtowns of our cities, and the high-rise housing projects towering over the old slums, looked cold and impersonal — like the centralized economy that produced them. Social critics said that we live in a technological society, where ordinary people are powerless. Environmentalists created a political movement dedicated to controlling destructive technologies.

In the 1970s, mid-century modernism was exhausted. The modernists' glass, steel, and concrete boxes, which had seemed so striking in the 1950s, were now anything but new and different. Serious postmodernists began to develop more humanistic architecture, while other architects searched for fresh novelties that could still shock and surprise people — beginning with the ironic side of postmodernism and leading to today's avant-gardism.

Our avant gardists produce futuristic architecture, like the early modernists, but are no longer capable of the social idealism of the early modernists. The political meaning has disappeared, because today's avant-gardist architects are not responding to the needs of our time in the way that the early modernists responded to the needs of the last century. A century ago, the modernist esthetic fit right in with the progressive goal of building a technological economy that could eliminate poverty and sweep away traditional forms of oppression. But now that this technophilia has faded, our avant-gardist architects create high-tech forms purely for the sake of novelty. They are not part of a larger progressive political movement, and they have no social ideal to give their forms meaning.

Modernism changed from a radical movement to the status quo because our society changed. The modernists criticized the traditional society of the early twentieth century in the name of technology and progress. But they have no critical insight into the new problems of today's technological society.

The task of our time is to use technology for human purposes. The avant garde tries to create totally new forms. It is so eager to reject that past that it rejects principles that were common to all traditional and vernacular architecture because evolution hardwired them into human nature. The avant gardists are not part of the broader progressive politics of our time, because they work against a key political task of our time, using technology in a way that is consonant with human nature.

Avant gardists as Conservatives

Today's avant gardists keep the esthetic dogmas of early modernism—its rejection of historic ornamentation and its search for strikingly original designs—but their buildings no longer symbolize any social ideal. Avant gardists sometimes play at being radical by claiming that their architecture is subversive, but their attempt to "subvert conventional ideas of what a building is" obviously have no effect at all on the real world of politics. They are just esthetes talking about subversion to other esthetes. They are not part of a larger movement to reform society, as mid-century modernist architects were.

In fact, avant gardism is the preferred style of our

technological corporate economy. It became clear decades ago that the glass high-rises of the mid-twentieth century modernists, far from being politically progressive, were symbols of the dominance of the modern corporation — towering over the city, expressing the power of the corporations that built them. And today's avant gardists have inherited the modernists' corporate clients.

London's skyline was marred by boxy modernist office buildings decades ago, and now it is being ruined by even larger avant-gardist office buildings with nicknames that describe their strange shapes, such as the "gherkin" and the "shard of glass." The mayor of London explained to a journalist why he wants to build more high-rises in this style: "In the global tussle between world metropolises for investment and jobs, he says, companies will choose London only if they can occupy 'signature buildings.'"[58] Despite their radical posturing, the avant gardists' high-rises are today's corporate architecture, just as boxy high-rises were the corporate architecture of mid-century.

The avant gardists' conservatism is most obvious on the rare occasions when they touch on real political issues — for example, when Ouroussoff talks about the beauty of cities built around the freeway. Freeway revolts were an important part of the progressive politics of the 1960s and the 1970s, and many progressive environmentalists today want to remove some existing freeways, but Ouroussoff is blissfully ignorant of the progressive urban politics of the last five decades.

This conservatism also pervades their work more deeply. Their designs express the idea that we should use any flashy new technology that is available, no matter how inhuman, at a time when progressives are trying to control destructive technologies.

Humanism as Social Change

Unlike the avant gardists, the New Urbanists are part of a powerful movement to reform society. Environmental groups across America support New Urbanism and smart growth in order to fight suburban sprawl, to conserve energy, and to slow global warming. When environmentalists in Portland wanted to stop the Western Bypass freeway, they got the New Urbanist planner, Peter Calthorpe, to draft a regional plan based on transit-oriented development, and they got other New Urbanists to design transit-oriented suburbs, such as Orenco Station.

The New Urbanists use models from the past, building developments that are like the railroad suburbs, streetcar suburbs, and urban neighborhoods of a century ago—and this is a real challenge to the modern economy, because it implies that Americans would be better off living more simply. Suburbia and freeways were mainstays of postwar American consumerism, and the New Urbanists are saying that we would be better off if we lived in homes that use less land and in neighborhoods where we have the choice of walking rather than being auto-dependent.

Environmentalists support New Urbanist design because it preserves open space and reduces energy consumption. The people who move to New Urbanist neighborhoods like them because they let you avoid the tension of driving in congested traffic on high-speed roads and because they have a stronger sense of community than sprawl suburbs.

If New Urbanist neighborhoods are more livable than conventional automobile-dependent suburbs, that fact is a real challenge to ExxonMobil, General Motors, and Wal-Mart—while the radical posturing of the avant gardists does not challenge the modern economy at all.

Choice of Technology

One young architecture student, angry to hear me support traditional styles, asked, "Would you design a computer to look like a quill pen?" Without realizing it, he raised an important point about choice of technology, and he revealed that architecture school indoctrinated him to ignore this point.

In some cases, new technologies clearly are better than old ones. No one wants to write with a quill pen rather than a computer. In these cases, it would obviously be dishonest to design the new technology to look like the old one.

In other cases, today's products use the same technologies as old ones. A new mirror, towel, or chest of drawers does not work differently from one made centuries ago. In these cases, it would be dishonest to design the old technology to look like something new—for example, to make it a chest of drawers that looks like a modernist sculpture.

In many cases, the most interesting ones, we need to make a choice of technology. Is it better to eat mass produced white bread or artisanal bread? To build freeways or walkable street grids in cities? To use chemical-intensive farming or organic farming? To use nuclear power or solar power? Often, the best option is somewhere between the two extremes: for example, we should move to use fewer chemicals in agriculture by using natural methods of controlling pests and weeds, but it is not realistic to shift to organic farming completely, because yield per acre is about 25% less without artificial nitrogen fertilizer. Sometimes, the old-fashioned way is clearly better: bread made with stone-ground whole wheat flour is healthier than bread made with chlorine-bleached white flour. Sometimes the new way is clearly better: using an automatic dishwasher is much easier than washing your dishes by hand.

Many architectural decisions involve this sort of choice of technology. Do we want to live in houses that look like glass boxes or in traditional houses? Do we want to live in superblocks with forty-story glass-and-steel apartment buildings or in traditional urban neighborhoods with six-story apartment buildings?

In the 1950s, people thought the modern method had to be better. Architects like Philip Johnson wanted to design homes that were glass boxes, and the general public wanted to eat mass-produced white bread.

Today, most people can see that the newest technology is not always the best. I am sure this architecture student would not insist on eating chemical food and say that eating organic food is like using like a computer designed to look like quill pen. I doubt if he would insist on building urban freeways and say that traditional street grids were like computers designed to look like quill pens. But he has been so indoctrinated in architectural modernism that he did insist on designing buildings in the modernist style for this strange reason.

We were talking about a five-story apartment building with a wood frame, not much different from apartment buildings of a century ago, so his argument obviously did not make sense. Yet he had been taught that, when it comes to architecture, all decisions about technology are like the computer and the quill pen. He had been taught that he should ignore choice of technology in his capacity as an architect, though he undoubtedly has more sense when it comes to food or urban design.

The Architect's New Clothes

To move forward, we must recognize that the emperors of today's architecture have no clothes.

The avant-gardists have immense pretensions and very little substance. Unlike the functionalists of a half-century ago, they have no larger social vision. Their empty catch phrases, obscure jargon, and artsy designs have captivated the academic elite. Their sensationalism has gotten them plenty of media coverage. But while they are creating artsy, sensational buildings, the humanists are doing the hard work of designing places that are good for people.

Modernism still made some sense in the early and mid twentieth century. Economic scarcity was still a key problem, as it had been all through human history, and modern industry promised to provide everyone with an adequate standard of living. Industrial food looked good compared with the days when people had trouble getting enough to eat, and high-rise housing projects looked good compared with the days when workers lived in tenements.

Modernism no longer makes sense today. America, as a whole, has moved beyond economic scarcity: we can afford better food than white bread and better homes than housing projects. We can focus on having a high quality of life rather than mass-produced essentials. At the same time, the environmental movement has taught us that we need to control dangerous technologies in order to maintain even a decent quality of life. Across the economy, we need to make a deliberate choice of technology, thinking about how to use technology in ways that protect nature and enhance human life.

Avant-gardists ignore this political issue of our time, the need to make good human use of technology. Their architecture is a perfect example of the superiority of technology over human values. Mid-twentieth century modernism seemed sterile and inhuman, and today's avant-gardists try so hard to be new and different that they seem deliberately anti-human. The fragmented and twisted forms of today's avant-gardist architecture, like Gehry's Stata Center or Libeskind's Denver Art Museum extension, symbolize the idea that we will do whatever technology makes possible—even if it makes people feel uncomfortable and disoriented.

What turns out to be "of our time" during the twenty-first century depends on the decisions we make about how we want to live.

Avant-gardist architecture is of our time in the sense that it represents the worst trends of our time. It represents a society devoted to sensationalism and novelty, where the media rush to cover anything that is new and different, marveling at how "cutting edge" the avant gardists' buildings are and never bothering to ask whether they are good places for people. It represents a fascination with technology that says, if we can do it, we should do it; new techniques of computer-aided design make it possible to build blob-shaped buildings, so we will build blob-shaped buildings—even if the people in them suffer from vertigo.

By contrast, humanistic architecture is of our time in the sense that it is contributing to a central task of our time, the task of making good human use of the possibilities that our technological society offers. If the humanists set the tone of our architecture and urbanism, then people will look back at the twenty-first century as the time when we learned how to use modern technology to design buildings and neighborhoods that are good places for people to live. If a larger humanistic movement sets the tone of our society generally, then we will move toward an economy that is sustainable and that provides a high quality of life.

There have been two times in the past when architecture has made a major contribution to the larger cultural change of its time. Renaissance architecture contributed to the revival of classical culture. Modernist architecture contributed to the rise of a technological society.

Today's architects can also make this sort of contribution by rejecting modernism in favor of humanistic architecture. Just as modernist architecture helped promote technophilia during the twentieth century, a humanistic architecture can help promote the focus on quality of life and human flourishing that we need in the twenty-first century.

Notes

1: Per capita GDP in 2005 dollars was $2,813.59 in 1870, $5,556.85 in 1900, and 39,749.59 in 2000. Louis Johnston and Samuel H. Williamson, "What Was the U.S. GDP Then?" MeasuringWorth, 2011. http://www.measuringworth.org/usgdp/. Poverty level in 2005 in the 48 contiguous states was $16,090 for a family of three, which comes to $5,363.33 per person. United States Department of Health and Human Services, *The 2005 HHS Poverty Guidelines*, http://aspe.hhs.gov/poverty/05poverty.shtml Thus, in 1900, average American income was just barely above what we now define as the poverty level, but it had almost doubled since 1870, raising the possibility that industrialization could raise the nation out of poverty.

2: John Kenneth Galbraith, *The Affluent Society* (Boston, Houghton Mifflin, 1958).

3: Christopher Alexander, *The Timeless Way of Building* (Oxford University Press, 1979).

4: Nikos Salingaros, *A Theory of Architecture* (ISI Distributed Titles, 2007) p. 30 et seq.

5: Jan Gehl, *Life Between Buildings: Using Public Spaces*, translated by Jo Koch (Washington, Island Press, 2011, first published in Danish in 1971) p. 156.

6: I trace the history of modernist theory of city planning briefly in this book. For a longer discussion, see my book Charles Siegel, *Unplanning: Livable Cities and Political Choices* (Preservation Institute, 2010).

7: Sigfried Giedion, *Space, Time and Architecture: the Growth of a New Tradition* (Cambridge, Mass., Harvard University Press, 1954) p. 744.

8: Clarence Perry, *Housing for the Machine Age* (New York, Russell Sage Foundation, 1939) p. 51. Perry emphasized this point: "If any of the original boundaries of a unit are not suited for through traffic, they should be widened by taking land, if necessary, from the unit area."(Perry, *Housing for the Machine Age*, p. 56).

9: "Wide and conspicuous boundaries enable residents and the public in general to see the limits of the community and visualize it as a distinct entity." Perry, *Housing for the Machine Age*, p. 472, p. 56-57.

10: Perry, *Housing for the Machine Age*, see map on p. 54.

11: Jane Jacobs, *The Death and Life of Great American Cities* (New York, Random House, 1961).

12: William H. Whyte, Jr., "Urban Sprawl," in The Editors of Fortune, *The Exploding Metropolis: A Study of the Assault on Urbanism and How Our Cities Can Resist It* (Garden City, New York, Doubleday Anchor, 1958) p. 115.

13: Oscar Newman, *Defensible Space: Crime Prevention through Urban Design* (New York, Macmillan, 1972). Though there have been criticisms of the methodology of this book, its basic thesis that modernist housing projects increased crime is indisputable, as evidenced by the adoption of the HOPE VI program.

14: Mark Hansen and Yuanlin Huang, "Road Supply and Traffic in Californian Urban Areas," *Transportation Research A*, Volume 31, No 3, 1997, pp. 205-218.

15: As of 2005, HOPE VI spent $5.8 billion in 446 federal block grants to be used for demolishing existing projects and building replacements. http://en.wikipedia.org/wiki/HOPE_VI

16: Charles Jencks, *The Language of Postmodern Architecture*, third enlarged edition (New York, Rizzoli International Publications, 1981, first edition published 1977) p. 9.

17: For a complete history of these two freeway removals, see http://www.preservenet.com/freeways/FreewaysEmbarcadero.html and http://www.preservenet.com/freeways/FreewaysCentral.html

18: Robert Caro, *The Power Broker: Robert Moses and the Fall of New York* (New York, Alfred A. Knopf, 1974) p. 707.

19: *ibid*. p, 742.

20: *ibid*. p. 706.

21: Peter Blake, *Form Follows Fiasco* (Boston and Toronto, Little Brown, 1977) p. 106.

22: Robert Moses, *Public Works: A Dangerous Trade* (New York, McGraw Hill, 1970) p. 133.

23: Giedion, *Space, Time and Architecture*, p. 735.

24: Richard P. Hunt, "Expressway Vote Delayed by City; Final Decision Is Postponed After 6-Hour Hearing." *New York Times*, December 7, 1962, cited in http://en.wikipedia.org/wiki/Lower_Manhattan_Expressway#cite_note-NYT19621207-1

25: Roberta Brandes Gratz, *The Battle for Gotham: New York in the Shadow of Robert Moses and Jane Jacobs* (New York, Nation Books, 2010) p. 87.

26: Paul Davidoff, "Advocacy and Pluralism in Planning," *Journal of the American Institute of Planners*, 31:4, 331-338, November, 1965. To link to this article: http://dx.doi.org/10.1080/01944366508978187

27: Robert Goodman, *After the Planners* (New York, Simon & Schuster, 1971) pp. 18-20.

28: Jencks, *Language of Postmodern Architecture*, pp. 106-107.

29: http://en.wikipedia.org/wiki/Sint_Antoniesbreestraat

30: See Andres Duany, Elizabeth Plater-Zyberk, and Jeff Speck, *Suburban Nation: The Rise of Sprawl and the Decline of the American Dream* (New York, Northpoint Press: a division of Farrar, Straus and Giroux, 2000) pp. 176-178.

31: For a description and illustrations of this proposal, see Peter Katz, *The New Urbanism: Toward an Architecture of Community* (New York, McGraw-Hill, 1994) pp. 164-168.

32: "We stand for the restoration of existing urban centers and towns within coherent metropolitan regions, the reconfiguration of sprawling suburbs into communities of real neighborhoods and diverse districts, the conservation of natural environments, and the preservation of your built legacy." The Charter of the New Urbanism, quoted in Peter Calthorpe and William Fulton, *The Regional City: Planning for the End of Sprawl* (Washington, Covelo, London, Island Press, 2001) p. 282.

33: For detailed information about this plan, see Peter Calthorpe, *The Next American Metropolis: Ecology, Community and the American Dream* (Princeton Architectural Press, 1993) p. 122 *et seq*.

34: The plan gave localities some flexibility about how to design this transit-oriented development. Towns had the choice of adopting the plan's standard zoning or of developing local zoning that would meet the plan's targets for housing and job growth.

35: Anthony Flint, *Wrestling with Moses: How Jane Jacobs Took On New York's Master Builder and Transformed the American City* (New York, Random House, 2009) p. 174.

36: Lindsay quotation from Flint, *Wrestling with Moses*, p. 177. The account of the hearing here is based on Flint and on Jane Jacobs' own account of her arrest in Roberta Brandes Gratz, *The Battle for Gotham: New York in the Shadow of Robert Moses and Jane Jacobs* (New York, Nation Books, 2010) pp. 315-319.

37: In his article "The Tall Office Building Artistically Considered," *Lippincott's Magazine* #57, March 1896, Sullivan wrote, "form ever follows function." The condensed phrase "form follows function" caught on among subsequent architects.

38: There is an English translation of this essay in Jean-Louis Ferrier and Yann le Pichon, *Art of Our Century: The Chronicle of Western Art, 1900 to the Present* (New York, Prentice-Hall, 1988).

39: Robert Venturi, *Complexity and Contradiction in Architecture* (New York, Museum of Modern Art, 2002, first published in 1977) p. 17.

40: Cited in Blake, *Form Follows Fiasco*, p. 10.

41: History of Friar's Quay from http://en.wikipedia.org/wiki/Friars_Quay_%28Norwich%29

42: Cited in Jencks, *Language of Postmodern Architecture*, p. 125.

43: http://en.wikipedia.org/wiki/Portland_Building

44: Bunny Wong, "The World's Ugliest Buildings" *Travel + Leisure*, October 2009.

45: Robert Venturi, Denise Scott Brown and Steven Izenour, *Learning from Las Vegas: The Forgotten Symbolism of Architectural*

Form, Revised Edition (Cambridge, MIT Press, 1977) p. 87 *et. seq.*

46: Both critics quoted in Robin Pogrebin, "Extreme Makeover: Museum Edition," *New York Times*, September 18, 2005.

47: Steve Bailey, "The $300m Fixer-Upper," *Boston Globe*, October 29, 2004, available at http://www.boston.com/business/articles/2004/10/29/the_300m_fixer_upper/

48: Cited by Laura Sydell "Balancing Form, Function In Museum Architecture," National Public Radio, December 08, 2008, http://m.npr.org/news/front/97965115?page=2&textSize=large

49: Robin Pogrebin, "Altered Spaces: The Good, the Bad, and the Dizzying," *New York Times*, March 28, 2007, p. H18.

50: Gwenda Blair, "White Elephant in Vermont Reincarnated," *New York Times*, October 10, 2002, House & Home section, pp. D1 and D4.

51: All quotations from Nicolai Ouroussoff, "Oscar Niemeyer, Architect Who Gave Brasília Its Flair, Dies at 104," *New York Times*, December 5, 2012. http://www.nytimes.com/2012/12/06/world/americas/oscar-niemeyer-modernist-architect-of-brasilia-dies-at-104.html?ref=obituaries

52: Nicolai Ouroussoff, "Outgrowing Jane Jacobs and Her New York," *New York Times*, April 30, 2006. http://www.nytimes.com/2006/04/30/weekinreview/30jacobs.html?_r=0

53: http://www.archnewsnow.com/features/Feature202.htm

54: Robert A.M. Stern, *Modern Classicism* (New York, Rizzoli, 1988) p. 187.

55: Jan Gehl, *Life Between Buildings*, p. 98.

56: Vancouver's density is 13,590/sq mi. http://en.wikipedia.org/wiki/Vancouver. Paris' density is 56,000/sq mi. http://en.wikipedia.org/wiki/Paris

57: One of the best examples is Le Plessis-Robinson, with a density of 67 people per acre. See Charles Siegel, "Le Plessis-Robinson: A Model for Smart Growth." planetizen.com, July 16, 2012.

58: Graham Bowley, "Mayor Tugs Sprawling London Up." *International Herald Tribune*, March 7, 2005.

www.ingramcontent.com/pod-product-compliance
Lightning Source LLC
Chambersburg PA
CBHW071718090426
42738CB00009B/1808